Deals And Discounts
If You're 50 or Older

Donna G. Albrecht

BRISTOL PUBLISHING ENTERPRISES, INC.
San Leandro, California

Printed in the United States of America.

ISBN 1-55867-032-7

Cover design: Frank Paredes
Back cover photography: Maxine Cass

CONTENTS

To Mike, for always believing in me —
— and to Katie and Abby for teaching me
the true meaning of perseverance.

CHAPTER 1:
AN INVITATION TO SAVE MONEY EVERY DAY

"Whoever said that money can't buy happiness didn't know where to shop."
- Author unknown

As prosaic as it may be, we all need money to buy those things we need — and many of the things that help us enjoy life more fully.

Since the government is very stuffy about letting us print our own money whenever we want more, it is important to get the most value for the money we spend.

At age 50, you became part of the fastest growing demographic segment in our nation. Because of your hard work, you and your peers in the U.S. already control 75 percent of the nation's wealth and half of its discretionary income. In fact, according to some sources, if you are now between the ages of 65 and 74, you have the highest percentage of discretionary income of any 10-year age group.

Businesses have not been blind to this trend. You have probably noticed that in the last few years, they have started to woo you through a variety of tactics.

Some have been more successful than others.

There have been a few spectacular flops like Gerber's Singles, pureed foods in baby food style jars for adult denture wearers, and Johnson & Johnson Inc.'s shampoo that was marketed for "old hair." Apparently, they failed to realize that today's 50+ consumer was more likely to be actively embracing life than rocking in a corner.

More savvy ways to attract your business have included hiring popular performers like Art Carney to pitch Coke Classic and Lena Horne and Rue McClanahan to promote Post Natural Bran Flakes.

Perhaps no marketing technique has been more successful than offering cash discounts. It is a win-win situation. The merchant attracts you to his or her store and you are able to buy items or services for less money than you would otherwise pay.

Everyone has heard that there are many discounts for mature consumers in the travel and hospitality (hotel, restaurant) arena. In recent years, there has been a quiet explosion in similar discounting programs in every imaginable place where you spend money. It has reached the point that if you are paying full price at the department store, drug store, photo studio, hardware store or almost anywhere else, you may be shopping at the wrong place.

As competition for your business grows, some businesses are trying to stand out from their competition by offering you everything from free health screenings to stimulating college-like classes.

In *Deals & Discounts*, I will show you thousands of ways to save money. Many of these opportunities are things you would have purchased even without the discounts. Others may be luxuries that you can buy because of the money you saved by using discounts on necessities.

In Oakley, California, Joann Nielsen tells the story about her husband, Bob, a dedicated discount user with a sense of humor. Recently, when Bob was checking out of the hardware store, the man behind him in line asked him why he asked for the 10 percent discount on a 20 cent item. He noted that Bob was wearing gold jewelry and did not appear to need the 2 cents. Bob turned around, smiled mischievously, and replied, "How do you think I buy my gold?"

USE IT OR LOSE IT

In my research for this book, I came across people who felt strongly that discounts should be based on need. They said that since many mature Americans do have significantly more discretionary income than younger people (who are struggling to bring up their families), discounts based on age are inappropriate.

Certainly, that is an important viewpoint. In a truly fair world, the discounts and breaks would always go to the people who needed them, regardless of age. Unfortunately, it is not a fair world. If you feel that you personally do not need a discount, there are ways you can help even things up.

First, remember that while the merchant may be offering you a discount because he believes you may need or deserve it, he is usually offering it to attract your business. If you do not take the discount, the merchant will not be donating the difference to charity.

However, if you do take the discount, you can choose to put aside that amount (maybe in a jar on your dresser) and every so often you can send the money to a charity you believe in. That way everyone wins, including the consumers who do need the benefits these discounts offer.

BOUQUETS OF ORCHIDS AND THISTLES

The people I talked to in researching this book gave me some insight into the things that merchants do which help or hinder the consumer's ability to find out about special age-related discount programs.

The bouquets of orchids go to those who advertise their programs and/or have special in-store displays to let you know what benefits are available to you. This makes it so much easier, especially for those who may not feel comfortable bringing the subject up to a clerk.

The blooming thistles (pretty flowers that come with nasty thorns) are reserved by some consumers for businesses which require you present their own discount card when you make a purchase.

We have all heard the stories about the person who whips out his wallet and shows 30 or 40 pictures of his grandchildren. In my research, I did not see many pictures of grandchildren, but I did see people whip out their wallets and show me packets of 30 or 40 discount cards. Each card was only good at one place.

From the merchant's standpoint, it does make sense to identify his customers. By signing up for his discount card, you are supplying him with a mailing list of motivated consumers he can send advertising materials to.

However, if merchants would let their consumers use an identification like their driver's license which gives their age, many would also be delighted to sign up for age-specific mailings. It would prevent a lot of bulging wallets and pockets — and maybe there would be a lot more pictures of grandchildren being carried around.

In all fairness, there are already many businesses which accept proof of age such as a driver's license or membership card in an organization like AARP as valid identification. There are also innovative programs like the Ohio Department of Aging's *Golden Buckeye Card* where one card is honored by thousands of merchants throughout the state (see Chapter 10).

Thistles (with no blooms) go to those people or firms who try to scare mature people into buying something they do not need and say they are giving a "discount" when they do it. Unfortunately, there are some people who will try to take advantage of those in the throws of retirement planning or other major life changes who may be concerned about their financial situation, personal health or safety. Remember, no discount is big enough if what you buy has no real value to you.

As you read this book, keep these other things in mind:

- **COMPARISON SHOP** There may be another offer from the same merchant that is a better deal. For instance, the "early bird" dinner at your favorite restaurant may cost less than a regular dinner with a senior discount. Few merchants will let you apply more than one discount to a purchase.

- **ASK FIRST** Always ask for your discount at the time when you make your reservations, make your purchase, or place your order. It may be too late if you wait until you are ready to pay your bill.

- **CHECK FOR RESTRICTIONS** The most obvious restriction is age. Many discount programs become available to you as soon as you turn 50; others may begin at 55, 60 or 65. Also, while many discounts are available whenever the business offering it is open, others may be restricted to certain days, hours, or times of the year.

- **CARRY IDENTIFICATION** Most of the time you will be asked for proof of your age (driver's license or state identification card if you do not drive), or proof of membership in an organization that sponsors the discount or the identification card issued by the discount provider.

- **VERIFY TERMS** All details about the discounts and deals included in this book were supplied by the companies and organizations which offer them. To the best of my knowledge, they were accurate at the time of publication. However, programs and terms can be changed at the discretion of those who offer them.

As you read the book, you will see many wonderful programs in the U.S. and Canada. The benefits mentioned in a chapter you are reading may make you curious about an overall program, minimum age, cost, etc. If so, just flip back to Chapter 11 where many of the membership groups are profiled. If you are interested in a membership group not covered in Chapter 11 (like the airline clubs), contact the address or phone number given in the chapter where the program was mentioned.

I would like to thank the many companies and organizations who responded to my inquiries about their programs. Although no individual, company or organization in any way sponsored this book, many have made an extra effort to supply me with background information about their programs to help me provide you with a clear understanding of how these programs work and what they can mean to you, my readers.

By using the information in *Deals & Discounts* you can save money every day. Whether you want to buy toiletries, get a haircut, refurnish your home or plan a dream vacation, this book is the tool that will help you save money on everything.

So —

> Get ready —
> Get set —
> Go have fun saving money!

CHAPTER 2:
SAVINGS ON FINANCIAL SERVICES/TAXES

"In God We Trust — All others pay cash."
- sign at a garage sale.

Do you remember the phrase, "Today is the first day of the rest of your life?" It has a way of reminding you that everything you do today will affect you for years to come.

Financial planning works that way, too. If you do not handle your finances carefully today, you may not have the assets you want and need in the future.

There are resources you can use to help you make the most of your money whether you are talking about millions or something less. The financial information breaks down into categories which sometimes overlap each other.

Those categories include financial planning, banking assistance, brokerage assistance and tax planning. At the end of this chapter, there is a chart you can use to help you organize your current expenses, income and net worth. If you are looking ahead to retirement, you can use it to work out what you will have then.

Some of the programs mentioned in this chapter include wonderful deals and discounts that you can benefit from. Other parts give information you can use to make the most of the money you have. Remember, you bear the ultimate responsibility for taking care of your own financial situation.

FINANCIAL PLANNING

When you were younger, financial planning meant saving a down payment for a house and putting aside money for your children's education. Now it involves analyzing your current assets, your retirement benefits, and working out plans to help you maximize your retirement income.

Plan to Succeed

According to the Institute of Certified Financial Planners (ICFP), the term "financial planning" has become a buzz phrase to describe the work of thousands of people. Unfortunately, a few of them are unscrupulous, so you need to be very careful when choosing a financial planner.

In the most basic sense, the purpose of working out a financial plan is to provide for the protection, accumulation and conservation of your assets. You do this through a combination of cash reserves, investment planning, insurance (especially on your life, income and possessions), tax planning, retirement planning, and estate planning.

With the complications that have arisen from tax "simplification," deregulation of the financial services industry, and a staggering array of financial products including IRA's, 401(k)'s, single-premium life, money markets, annuities and other investment choices, you may decide you want professional help to create the financial plan that best suits your assets, lifestyle and future needs.

One person who can help you is a professional financial planner. You can ask your lawyer or accountant for a recommendation of planners they know who regularly work with people in your income bracket. Another way is to call the Institute of Certified Financial Planners at 1-800-282-PLAN and they will give you a list of Certified Financial Planner practitioners in your area. You may want to talk to several before choosing the person you feel most comfortable working with. As you would in any business relationship of this type, ask for the names of clients who you can call as references — then call them.

The ICFP wants you to know that most states have requirements for investment advisers, including financial planners. On the federal level, ICFP recommends that anyone calling himself or herself a financial planner be a Registered Investment Adviser with the Securities & Exchange Commission and with the state securities agency when appropriate. This will help protect you from unethical practitioners.

The planner should be willing to give you a full disclosure in writing. This disclosure should include his or her resume (showing education and experience), the type of work done, method of compensation, and current or potential conflicts of interest. You should have this written disclosure before you contract with the planner for his services.

In addition, financial planners must be licensed for specific financial services they provide such as selling stocks and bonds, insurance products, or real estate. Check with the appropriate state licensing agencies and the Securities & Exchange Commission to verify the planner's credentials. Even if making the calls leaves you feeling foolish, it is not nearly as bad as you would feel if you found later you had chosen a planner who was not what he presented himself to be.

How They Are Paid

There are three ways your planner may be compensated. If you have chosen your planner carefully, the way he is compensated should not have any impact on your planning. If someone seems to be pressing you to purchase a financial product he will earn a commission on, and you do not feel it is in your best interest, find another planner.

The three ways your financial planner could earn compensation are: fees (based on an hourly rate or the value of your assets and/or income); fees and commissions (if you purchase any financial products suggested by the planner which he or she earns a commission on); and commissions (some planners earn only from sales of insurance and/or investments).

Once you have developed a financial plan, you will need to review it regularly. Once a year, maybe right after you file your tax return, meet with your planner to be sure your plan is keeping up with changes in your financial situation. Along with the annual review, ICFP has these other tips to help you make the most of your financial planning relationship:

- Do not give your financial planner "carte blanche" to wheel and deal with your money. Stay involved at all times.

- Make sure your investments match your tolerance for risk.

- Read all statements regarding your finances. Read insurance documents, bank statements, investment updates, stock market reports and annual shareholder information.

- Update your planner whenever you experience a change in your financial situation (lump-sum retirement fund disbursements, moving to a new home, etc.)

- Call your planner whenever you have a question. If he is annoyed by this, find a new planner.

BANKING

Special discounts and services have long been a staple at banks as well as savings and loan organizations.

However, if Peter Levine of Plantation, Florida is successful, these deals and discounts will soon be a part of the past. In early 1990, he filed a complaint with the Human Relations Department of Broward County, Florida against the C&S Bank because of the special programs they offered people 55 or older.

Within 90 days, the bank offered him a settlement which would have entitled him to the same benefits as a 55-year-old, even though he was a decade younger. This settlement included provisions for confidentiality, which meant he could not talk about the case for publication.

Levine declined the offer because of the confidentiality clause and Broward County closed the case because of his failure to accept what they termed "full relief." The C&S Bank declined to comment on the case.

Levine feels strongly that special "senior" discounts are illegal because they involve age discrimination. He says he favors discounts like "early-bird dinners" because they are available to everyone. So far his case is strictly a matter of his conscience, and he is funding his own legal matters. In mid-1990, he was appealing the decision and considering filing a law suit against the county.

Until or unless Levine is successful, you can still get great benefits through many banks or other financial institutions. These deals and discounts are an unbeatable way to improve your own financial situation.

As you check with your local financial institutions, you will probably find many similarities in the benefits they offer. Those benefits may become fairly standardized if the Richer Life Program, offered by Value Added Marketing in Massachusetts, continues to gain acceptance. Richer Life is marketed to financial institutions, giving them a complete program that is ready to offer their patrons.

President Robert Collins says that the program is based on research into the wants and needs of these consumers. The kinds of benefits (all free to the consumer) Richer Life offers include: Now Checking with personalized checks; money orders and traveler's checks; accidental death and common carrier insurance; investment counseling; trust consultation; seminars on financial issues; and a newsletter.

One thing that sets it apart from programs which only offer free or discounted banking services is that there is a strong social aspect to Richer Life. There is a regular schedule of bank-coordinated social and travel activities for members to participate in.

For instance, during the first year it was offered at Bank Five For Savings in Burlington, Massachusetts, members had the opportunity to participate in four cocktail parties, four dinner/theater parties, an investment seminar and trips to New York and Bermuda.

The big kick-off event began with bank officers serving hors d'oeurves and champagne before they left on a group trip to see the Nutcracker Suite performed in Boston. Richer Life is certainly changing the staid, dour face of banking and making the whole idea of banking a lot more fun.

Marie Rittman, assistant vice president of marketing for Bank Five For Savings says that while there are many financially-based benefits, the big draw is the social and travel benefits members enjoy. It has made the program so popular that they have hired a group coordinator to handle the monthly events.

At Bank Five, membership in Richer Life is free to anyone age 50 or older who has $20,000 on deposit. That money can be distributed in any combination of savings, checking, NOW, and IRA's or Certificates of Deposit. Bank customers with smaller total deposits can join by paying a $10 per month fee. However, Rittman notes that nearly all the members have at least the minimum deposit, and the average balance of these members is $67,000.

Value Added Marketing's Collins mentions that the program may go by different names, since many banks, savings & loans, credit unions, etc. who are a part of Richer Life, personalize the name of the program for their clients. Collins expects the program to expand nationally by 1991 and be available in Canada soon. To find out if there is a financial institution near you which offers this plan, you can call 1-800-234-7111.

Many financial institutions have developed their own programs. They involve free or discounted financial services, but you will need to shop carefully — there are some substantial differences between them.

At BancOhio National Bank in Ohio, customers age 55 or older can take advantage of their special package offering unlimited standard personalized checks (200 per order), no-fee traveler's checks and the ability to pay certain utility bills at no charge. By choosing their Classic 55 Checking Account, you would not have to pay any regular service charges and there is no minimum balance or maximum number of transactions.

You would also have to be 55 to use the Renaissance Banking program at First Chicago, but aside from the checking accounts with no per-check fees and no minimum balance, the conditions of the program are very different. Your *first* order of checks is free.

Your benefits with this bank also include interest on your checking account, emergency cash advance service, nationwide check cashing privileges and overdraft protection (if you qualify).

In addition, you will find a lot of interesting freebies. You can have a safe deposit box free for one year, no-fee traveler's checks purchased at First Chicago, and no annual fee on First Chicago Visa or MasterCard (if you qualify).

At Central Bank of the South one of the benefits available starting at age 50 is a new Visa or MasterCard (subject to credit approval, of course); however, the annual fee is only waived for the first year. At Central Bank there are some other attractive benefits for customers of their Applause Account. They are like many other institutions with their offer of no-fee traveler's checks, discount on a safe deposit box and free personalized checks, etc. However, if you like to keep your funds in Certificates of Deposit, Central Bank's ¼ percent CD bonus rate could be the feature that brings you to them.

There are other institutions which have special CD rates and/or terms to encourage you to do business with them. At Continental Savings of America in California, they have a special Super Senior Silver Certificate for those 60 and over. Customers can lock in the rate for 12 months and invest with a minimum deposit of $1,000.

A FULL BENEFIT PACKAGE

Like the Richer Life program mentioned earlier, some financial institutions offer such a wonderful package of benefits that banking there is a lot like joining a club.

If you live in the Southeast, First Union Benefit Banking is a tremendous program. If you live somewhere else, ask around to find out if any local bank, credit union or savings & loan can give you a similar great deal.

Beginning at age 55, First Union Benefit Banking members can take advantage of a number of services including free checks, interest on your checking account, discounted safe deposit box, bonus interest on Certificates of Deposit and no-fee travelers cheques, money orders, official checks and notary service.

Then they add on the benefits which broaden Benefit Banking to a whole different level. At no additional charge, you will receive $100,000 of travel accident insurance when you travel on any type of common carrier. Again, at no additional charge, you will receive $1,000 of accidental death insurance per account, and you can even take advantage of a low annual membership fee on a buying service that provides savings on merchandise, travel services and prescription drugs. Wow!

And that's not all. There are additional options which are available to you as a Benefit Banking member. Some of these fascinating options are:

- A toll-free insurance line where specialists can answer your questions, provide advice and offer you insurance protection in areas including life, health, automobile and homeowners.

- Mutual funds (both load and no load) designed to meet your individual investment goals.

- Personal trust services through their Capital Management Group which offers professional investment management, estate administration, trust administration, custodian services, real estate management and IRA Rollover trusts (standard fees apply).

- Discount brokerage for those who prefer to make their own investment decisions and save on commissions.

All the benefits of the Benefit Banking program can be yours if you are 55 or older, meet one of several minimum balance options, or pay a flat monthly fee of $7.

A similar program called Club 55 is available to customers at Citizens Fidelity Bank & Trust Company in Kentucky and Indiana. Club 55 has some exciting benefits that are usually only found through major programs including preferred rate installment loans, discount pharmacy service, key ring protection, a financial newsletter, credit card protection and discounts on travel and recreation.

Like some large membership organizations, Club 55 even offers members a cash bonus of five percent on airline travel, cruises, lodging, car rental and package trips. As a member, you can get this bonus whenever you travel, whether it is for business or pleasure.

Since new tax laws and financial products can make your banking experience a challenge, the idea of having a personal banker like you use to find in your neighborhood bank is a real attraction. At Bank One's 670 offices in Indiana, Kentucky, Michigan, Ohio, Texas and Wisconsin, each bank assigns one or more persons to be full-time Senior Champs coordinators. This coordinator's responsibilities can range from making sure you are receiving the services you deserve to arranging seminars, trips, events and social functions.

To access Senior Champs, you must be 55 years old. There is also a required deposit of $5,000 in a combination of Certificates of Deposit or savings products. They offer interest paying checking accounts with no service charge and free checks (of course), and an informative newsletter. You can choose to use the mail-order pharmacy service they offer, attend educational seminars and save money traveling through the special package prices and travel opportunities.

These kinds of benefits are certainly worth a little extra research on your part. The wide range of programs mentioned above will give you an idea of what benefits you can expect to find in your area.

Remember the key word here is "ask." No matter where you live, it is likely that some financial institution is offering special deals and discounts to help you save money on your financial transactions. If your favorite financial institution is not offering you a deal, talk with the president and explain the benefits — and why people like you are moving their deposits to institutions which offer these benefits.

BROKERAGE ASSISTANCE

The ability to buy and sell stock is a critical factor in helping business grow in a free market economy. The stock market can justifiably take credit for helping create the affluent lifestyle enjoyed by so many today.

Yet, investing in the stock market can be complicated and not a little scary, since it is your future you are gambling with. If you have been investing for some time, you probably already have a stock broker who works with you — or perhaps you are comfortable making your own decisions without counseling and prefer a discount brokerage.

However, you may find yourself suddenly put in a position where you have a sum of money and want to invest it. Maybe you find yourself with or expecting a lump-sum retirement distribution of hundreds of thousands of dollars. Maybe you are 55 or older and are taking advantage of the capital gains exclusion for $125,000 when you sell you home, giving you a large sum you want to invest for future needs. Maybe you have just moved to a new community and want to find a good stockbroker.

Vice President and Retirement Planning Coordinator Bob Burke of Dean Witter in Walnut Creek, California, has some tips for you. He suggests that you call the office manager of several well-known firms, explain your needs, and ask for a referral in their office. He says that way you are most likely to get a stockbroker who will work well for you. Burke adds that when people just walk in off the street, they are more likely to be referred to the least busy (and least experienced) brokers because they happen to have some time available right then.

Burke mentions that Dean Witter has a free service that could benefit anyone age 50 or older who is dealing with retirement planning. The service is called Pre-Retirement Income Management Evaluator (PRIME). You begin by filling in the confidential questionnaire which you can get at any Dean Witter office.

The questionnaire includes questions about all your investments, employer-sponsored retirement plans and pensions and Social Security benefits. When you have completed the form, it is sent to a central office where professionals evaluate your programs and determine what you need to do to meet your retirement income goals.

An account executive (yours if you have one) will go over the report with you to be sure you understand it. Your account executive will suggest ways to help you meet your goals, but all the decisions about when or whether to implement the plan are yours.

This free service is a great offer, especially if your situation is complicated and you are wondering what your actual retirement income will be. Using PRIME does not obligate you to use Dean Witter services — but they would probably be delighted to give you any help you want with your brokerage needs.

As you check with different brokerage houses, you will find they each are making an effort to attract your business. (Remember the introduction to this book: you and your peers control a lot of wealth).

You will see a lot of advertising by companies such as Dreyfus offer to help you consolidate your IRAs. Each firm will have its strengths, and some of them may meet your needs better than others. Take time to investigate the firm you are considering working with. After all, it is your money.

Be sure you understand not only the amount of return you can expect, but the risk you may be taking. You may be able to buy Certificates of Deposit which are insured by the FDIC at the same place you can buy mutual fund shares which are not guaranteed by anyone.

Another place to look for some assistance may be a group you already belong to.

AARP has an investment program from Scudder, Stevens & Clark with a toll-free phone number. A few of the benefits include IRA accounts with no start-up or custodial fees, low initial investments, consolidated statements, direct deposit of Social Security and other regular income checks and even a toll-free TDD line for the hearing and speech impaired.

National Association for Retired Credit Union People (NARCUP) members can get quality brokerage services at discount prices through Direct Brokerage Services, which is a service of the Pershing Division of Donaldson, Lufkin and Jenrette Securities Corporation.

The National Alliance of Senior Citizens (NASC) also offers various mutual funds which are managed by Federated Securities Corporation. Other benefits include professional money management.

Certainly, there must be many other groups which offer some level of investment services to members. If this option interests you, check the information packet you received when you joined the group(s) you are in or write or call the main office.

TAX PLANNING

Tax planning can be terribly complex, even if your finances are fairly simple. It can be worth the work, though, when you find ways to save money.

The following tips are only to give you an idea of some of the ways you can save money on your taxes because of your status as what the IRS calls an "Older American." Because of space limitations (and constantly changing regulations), this section does not include all the information on each benefit. Contact your tax advisor or the IRS for further details and clarification on how these programs apply to your individual situation.

You may call or visit your local IRS office which is listed in the white pages of your phone book under U.S. Government. They have a wealth of information available to you in the form of free publications. Three you may be especially interested in are Publication 554, *Tax Information for Older Americans*; Publication 524, *Credit for the Elderly or the Disabled*; and Publication 523, *Tax Information on Selling Your Home*.

The good news is that there are four specific tax benefits available to older Americans. One of these benefits applies to all taxpayers 65 or older. (You are considered 65 on the day before your 65th birthday. It is the government's rule — it does not have to make sense.) The other three benefits are available only to those who qualify. The benefit everyone 65 or older qualifies for is a special gross income requirement for filing a federal income tax return. This benefit is available if you file Form 1040 or Form 1040A.

If you and/or your spouse qualify and meet the age requirement, you may benefit from a tax credit for the elderly or the disabled. The maximum credit available is $1,125 which you may be eligible for if you are 65 or older or retired on disability and were permanently and totally disabled when you retired. This is a little complicated, but it is explained in Publication 524, previously mentioned.

One benefit if you are age 55 or older is the opportunity to exclude up to $125,000 ($62,500 if you are married filing separately) of gain when you sell your home. You can exclude from your gross income part or all of the gain from the sale of your main home, if you meet certain age, ownership, and use tests at the time of the sale. Unfortunately, you can choose to exclude gain only once for sales after July 26, 1978.

The earliest date on which you can sell your home

and still qualify for the exclusion is your 55th birthday (no extra day early here). You must have owned and used the home as your main home for three of the five years ending on the date of the sale — but those three years do not have to be continuous. Short temporary absences for vacations, or other seasonal absences, even if you rent out the property during the absences, are counted as periods of use. There are also some exceptions for people who become disabled. You can only use this gain exclusion once. If you or your spouse chose to exclude gain from a sale after July 26, 1978, neither of you can choose to exclude gain again for a sale after that date.

If you and your spouse each owned separate homes before your marriage and sold both homes after your marriage, you can exclude the gain on one of them, but not on both. (So if you are contemplating marriage and you both own a home, you may want to look into selling both homes before you are married, each taking the exclusion, and then buying another home together.)

If after choosing to exclude gain, you and your spouse divorce, neither of you can exclude gain again If you remarry, you and your new spouse cannot exclude gain on sales after your marriage. However, you can revoke a previous choice under certain circumstances (it is very complicated; check it out with your tax advisor).

The fourth tax benefit you may be eligible for is an increase in your standard deduction. If you do not itemize deductions, you are entitled to a higher standard deduction as long as you are 65 or older on the last day of the tax year (once again you get the bonus day — you are considered 65 on the day before your birthday).

As complex as taxes are, you do not have to face the job of figuring them out by yourself. Many people take advantage of the fact that the IRS will figure your tax under certain circumstances. You can call your local office for the specific instructions for the kind of form (1040EZ, 1040, 1040A) which you expect to file.

Once again, groups you belong to may have special benefits to help you with your tax preparation. Montgomery Ward's Y.E.S. membership includes a 10 percent discount off the regular rate on both long and short forms at their in-store tax preparation service between February 1 and April 15.

Check with your local senior citizen's center. Accountants in your area who specialize in working with mature taxpayers may offer special discounts through the center.

Also, check with other professional tax services to see what they offer. Many (but not all) H&R Block offices in the U.S. and Canada offer discounts on the work they do for mature taxpayers.

NET WORTH CALCULATIONS

This simple chart can help you determine your current financial situation and what it could be in the future. There is even a handy Inflation Impact Table to assist you in determining what you will need at retirement or some other point in the future.

Assets/Liabilities

Assets	Now	At Retirement
Savings Accounts		
Checking Accounts		
Time Deposits		
U.S. Savings Bonds		
Life Insurance (cash value)		
Annuities (surrender value)		
Pension (vested interest)		
Investments (market value)		
House (market value)		
Other Real Estate (market value)		
Business Interests		
Personal Property (auto, etc.)		
Other Assets		
TOTAL ASSETS	$	$

Liabilities	Now	At Retirement
Mortgage (balance due)		
Automobile Loan		
Installment Loans		
Taxes Due		
Business Debts		
TOTAL LIABILITIES	$	$

Subtract total liabilities from total assets:

	Now	At Retirement
Total Assets	$	$
Total Liabilities	$	$
NET WORTH	$	$

26

INCOME/OUTGO

Income	*Now*	*At Retirement*
Salary		
Your Own:		
Your Spouse's:		
Commissions		
Tips		
Bonuses		
Interest		
Dividends		
Rental Property		
Royalties		
Social Security		
Pension Benefits		
Profit-Sharing		
Annuities		
Life Insurance Benefits		
Other		
TOTAL INCOME	$	$

Outgo	Now	At Retirement
Housing (rent, mortgage payments)		
Household Maintenance (fuel, utilities, etc.)		
Food (meals home & out)		
Clothing		
Transportation		
Medical/Dental Care		
Insurance Premiums		
Life		
Health		
Homeowner's		
Automobile		
Taxes		
Income		
Property		
Entertainment/Recreation		
Charitable Giving		
Personal/Miscellaneous		
TOTAL OUTGO	$	$
Total Income	$	$
Total Outgo	$	$
DIFFERENCE (+ or −)	$	$

INFLATION WORKSHEET

How Much Will You Need in Retirement?

	Current Expenses	Est. Retirement Expenses
Food		
Housing		
Transportation		
Clothing		
Medical		
Savings & Investments		
Life Insurance		
Other		
TOTAl		

PROJECTION FOR INFLATION

Multiply the total from the step above by the appropriate inflation factor from the Inflation Impact Table below. For example, if you are five years from retirement (or the year you are targeting) you will use Inflation Factor 1.4024 to learn how much you will actually need that first retirement year. After that, project for five years into retirement and make any other projections you think are necessary.

Your first
retirement year:_____

Five years
after retirement:_____

Further
projections: _____   _____

INFLATION IMPACT TABLE
(Compounded at 7% per year)

Year	Inflation	Year	Inflation	Year	Inflation
1	1.0700	11	2.1042	21	4.1434
2	1.1449	12	2.2514	22	4.4334
3	1.2250	13	2.4117	23	4.7437
4	1.3107	14	2.5805	24	5.0757
5	1.4024	15	2.7611	25	5.4310
6	1.5005	16	2.9543	26	5.8112
7	1.6055	17	3.1611	27	6.2179
8	1.7178	18	3.3823	28	6.6532
9	1.8380	19	3.6191	29	7.1189
10	1.9666	20	3.8724	30	7.6172

This worksheet is courtesy of The American Council of Life Insurance.

CHAPTER 3: DISCOUNTS FROM MAJOR RETAILERS

"I'll make him an offer he can't refuse."
*Mario Puzo, **The Godfather**, 1969*

The key to keeping money in your pocket is saving money at stores where you shop regularly. That can include department stores, hardware stores and other places where you buy the clothes, furniture, tools and other things you need for yourself or your home.

Not surprisingly, many well-known retailers have recognized your buying power and offer everything from cash discounts to "clubs" which can include a wide array of discounts and services.

In addition to your buying power, they know that more than two-thirds of people age 50 or older are likely to be loyal to retailers who offer the best prices. Two old favorites, Montgomery Ward and Sears & Roebuck offer what are probably the largest, most elaborate programs.

At Montgomery Ward, Y.E.S. members are entitled to a 10 percent discount on all regular and sale merchandise every Tuesday. There is no minimum — or maximum — purchase you need to make. They do restrict the discount somewhat in that you cannot use it at their clearance outlets, repair services, food services or for merchandise purchased through the mail. It is also not valid in license departments or for auto service (where separate Y.E.S. discounts apply).

There are some other kinds of restrictions which you will find are pretty much common sense. The 10 percent discount cannot be applied to the sales tax, and it cannot be used against charges for delivery, installation or for service contracts.

However, that still leaves a lot of discount available. As long as you shop on Tuesday and carry the Discount Pass from the membership magazine *Vantage*, you will be able to give yourself a discount on everything from a dress for your granddaughter to a living room full of furniture.

Montgomery Ward also recognizes that getting out to the store can be difficult for some people with disabilities. While their discount is not available on mail-order merchandise, they have arranged to offer disabled Y.E.S. members the option of having a designated shopper who can make discounted purchases for them.

You can arrange to have this benefit by calling their customer service representatives at 1-800-421-5396. You will need a note from your doctor attesting to your need for this help, and you will have to have decided who your designated shopper will be so the information can be put in their records.

The Y.E.S. program has a membership fee of $2.90 per month which can be billed automatically to your credit card. Membership has other benefits, many of which are covered more fully in other chapters. Some of these benefits include:

- A subscription to *Vantage* magazine

- No-fee travelers checks
- Travel services and rebates for transportation, car rental and lodging
- Discounts at Montgomery Ward
  - -hair salons
  - -florists by phone
  - -free gift wrapping
  - -engraving services
  - -income tax preparation at in-store centers (Feb. 1 through April 15)
- Discounts on U.S. Sprint
- Discounts on personal needs for
  - -pharmacy by mail
  - -optical 20% on prescription lenses, frames and contact lenses at in-house optical centers
  - -hearing aids at their in-store centers or rebates at Beltone centers
- Discounts on other magazine subscriptions
- Photo Vision (transfer photos, home movies, etc. to video tape)

Whew! And that is just for one major retailer.

ARE YOU MATURE ENOUGH FOR THIS DEAL?

Sears Roebuck offers their own program called *Mature Outlook*. Probably with more sense of public identification with their name than editorial originality, their magazine is called *Mature Outlook* as well. They offer a wide array of services, especially targeting people who travel a lot.

You will get your choice of four (count 'em, 4!) discount programs for car rentals at Budget/Sears Rent a

Car, National Car Rental, Hertz Rent a Car and Avis Rent a Car. Benefits include travel accident insurance ($5,000 each for you and your spouse), traveler's checks, automatic membership in TravelAlert and room and restaurant discounts at Holiday Inns and Holiday Inn Crowne Plaza Hotels. As a member you are also eligible for 10 percent off the membership fee for the Allstate Motor Club.

Looking for a new or used car? Mature Outlook members can get the normal $20 charge for a print-out from Car/Puter reduced to $12 (plus $2 postage and handling). This detailed computerized print-out shows the Manufacturer's Suggested Retail Price and Dealer's Factory Invoice cost for the base car and all options, giving you the information you need to negotiate a better deal for yourself.

Like Ward's, Sears' program offers optical benefits. Mature Outlook members can chose to join Vision One and save up to 50 percent on eyewear products at participating locations (about 600) of the Optical Department at Sears. The cost for joining Vision One is also discounted. In early 1990, the regular annual fee was $21.95, but Mature Outlook members paid only $12.

However, Mature Outlook members do not have to join Vision One to get a discount. They are automatically eligible for a 20 percent savings on regular, non-sale prices of frames, prescription lenses and contact lenses at participating locations of the Optical Department at *Sears*. After this prodigious list of benefits, you may be wondering if there is any discount in the store.

There is.

When you pay the annual membership fee of $9.95,

they send you a coupon book worth $100. These coupons come in varying denominations and are good for Sears' services and retail or catalog purchases. The denominations begin at $2, which can be applied to purchases of $30 or more, and go up to $25, which can be applied to purchases of $375 or more. They cannot be used with any other offer or coupon, are non-transferable and, of course, cannot be used as payment on a SearsCharge or Discover Card account.

OTHERS MAJOR RETAILERS
MAKE DISCOUNTS TOO

Throughout this country, there are department stores which offer high quality, name-brand merchandise at discount prices. They tend to be very aware of what their consumers want and try to meet your expectations.

Venture Stores, with 76 department stores in Missouri, Illinois, Kansas, Oklahoma, Arkansas, Indiana and Kentucky, has been offering a discount program to their mature shoppers since 1983. Anyone age 62 or older can receive a 10 percent discount on everything (tobacco products, if available, may be excepted) they purchase on Wednesdays — every Wednesday of the year.

To access that discount, all you need to do is bring your valid driver's license or state identification card to the customer service desk and apply for their store identification card.

F.W. Woolworth and Woolworth Express offer you a smiliar program if you are 62 or older. Again, they take pity on the bulge in your pocket and do not require special identification. Your driver's license, state I.D. card or other proof of age is all you need.

The ten percent discount is offered one day a week, usually Tuesday. You can use the discount on everything in the store except tobacco and alcoholic beverages. To save time, their spokesperson reminds you to show your identification before the clerk starts ringing up your transaction.

Covering 20 states in the East and Midwest (plus Florida), Ames Department Stores are also trying to show how much they value your business by offering a discount to shoppers who are 60 or older.

This program offers shoppers 10 percent off unadvertised merchandise (except alcohol and tobacco products) one day each week. The day of the week it is offered will vary by store, so you will need to check with your local store customer service desk to find out when the discount is available in your town. While you are there, be sure to apply for your Senior Discount Card.

NOT EVERY DEAL IS BASED ON CASH (COMPLETELY)

Lots of people go to department stores to shop (no surprise there) and some go to socialize. Did you ever think of going to a department store to learn something completely new? There is a program called Older Adult Service & Information System (OASIS) which has the May Company as its largest sponsor. It is an educationally based program featuring classes on cultural topics and wellness. Many of the classes take place in space donated by the local May Company stores.

The program originated in 1982 as a pilot project in St. Louis. It was designed to reach out to people age 60 or older who were not interested in the activities at the traditional senior centers. These people enjoyed socializing with others their age, but also wanted the mental stimulation that comes from learning new skills.

Serving 92,000 members in 20 cities coast to coast, OASIS offers classes in subjects like creative writing, painting, sculpturing, and wellness lifestyle classes. The classes range from serious topics such as "Earthquakes and the New Madrid Fault" to the whimsical "Ornamental Yard Art," an academic study of research on artifacts of ornamental yard art from Missouri.

There is no membership fee for OASIS, but some classes may charge a nominal $1 per class meeting to help defray expenses.

Also, while the program does not offer travel benefits in the sense of being a travel agency, it does offer members an opportunity to join in on preplanned trips.

Ah! But how about discounts? The spokesperson for the OASIS program says that while this program is one of the best bargains around (think what these classes could cost through your local college), there are occasionally discounting privileges. Information on finding an OASIS site is in Chapter 11.

Discounting is most likely to happen in late November or early December. If the local May Store (like Famous Barr stores in the St. Louis area) offers a special discount day to mature shoppers (often 10 to 20 percent), then OASIS members may be offered an additional discount by that store.

HARDWARE STORES ARE SOFTIES
WHEN IT COMES TO A DEAL

Are hardware stores someplace you go when you need a specific doodad, or are they somewhere you go to browse around all the fascinating gadgets and ponder what you would do with them?

You may keep an eye on their ads to save money, but sometimes you can save even more than you think. Savvy hardware stores go even further and offer discounts to their mature shoppers.

Customers age 60 or older can get a 10 percent discount on all regular priced merchandise at participating Coast to Coast Total Hardware and Coast to Coast Home and Auto stores in 38 states.

Once again, the key word is "participating." There are approximately 1,200 Coast to Coast stores and they are franchised to the owners. This means that individual store owners make the decision whether they will offer this discount or not. Since Coast to Coast only initiated its discount program in June of 1988, your local store may not be participating yet. If not, let the owner know you are interested.

A spokesperson for Ace Hardware Corporation describes their corporation as a franchise organization structured from the bottom up. This means that the corporate office does not define programs like mature shopper discounts for the franchisees. Each store owner who chooses to have a program defines it himself. The offers range from a one-day-a-year discount to a 10 percent discount all year long.

Ten years ago at both Schauer's Ace Hardware stores in Chicago, owner Rich Schauer noticed that his stores had many mature shoppers, and some of them were asking if he offered senior discounts.

He decided to put his customers' interest together with two business factors. First, his slowest day of the week from a business standpoint was Wednesday. Second, he already offered commercial customers who purchased over $50 per month a 10 percent discount.

While he decided the discount for mature shoppers did not require a minimum purchase, he also decided that it would not be available on sale merchandise. Now, he says that thanks to the mature customers who come in to shop on Wednesdays, it is no longer the slowest day of the week.

Schauer notes that a few of his older customers will even try to avoid the crowds on Wednesday by coming in on Tuesday, picking out their merchandise, putting it in a small basket, and then hiding it in some nook or cranny in the store.

He says that his employees always straighten up his stores and restock the shelves every evening before going home. Shortly after starting the discount program, the employees began noticing these hidden caches of merchandise and putting the items away — much to the consternation of their customers in the morning.

Now, he says, they recognize the places where customers seem to prefer to hide things and they leave misplaced merchandise there until Thursdays — when it is usually gone. Schauer does add though, that it is a lot easier for his staff if customers just ask someone at the customer service desk to hold the basket until the next day.

CRAFTY SHOPPERS FIND BENEFITS

Admittedly, a hardware store is not everyone's idea of a great place to browse and shop for hobby items. However, 68 percent of you occasionally or regularly engage in hobbies at home.

Crafts & More has supplies for people who enjoy creating hand-made crafts. They have both free-standing stores and operate as a department in some Ames Department Stores. Like the other members of the Ames family, they offer mature shoppers who are at least age 60, a 10 percent discount on unadvertised merchandise every day.

BOOK THE DEAL YOU WANT

If you have gotten this far, then it is a sure thing that you enjoy reading. How would you like a chance to save money on books without having to commit to buying a certain number of books through a club?

At over 1,300 Waldenbooks, Preferred Readers members can receive a 10 percent discount on virtually every item in the store — even sale items! The only things excluded from the discount are magazines, newspapers and gift certificates. If you are under age 60, you can join the Preferred Reader Club for an annual fee of $10. Then, once you turn 60, you only pay a one-time fee of $10 for a lifetime membership.

When you present your club card at any Waldenbooks, the total of your purchase will be credited to your computerized account. Then, every time your accumulated purchases total $100, you will be mailed a $5 coupon good on a future purchase of $5 or more.

As a Preferred Reader member, you will receive other

useful benefits. Your membership card can be used as identification when you write a check (so you do not need to bring your license and credit card). Better yet, your membership entitles you to call a special toll-free phone number and order any books you want sent to you for the cost of the book and a minimal handling charge. This can be especially helpful if you live in a rural area or find that your health or responsibilities as a caretaker make it difficult for you to get out.

That toll-free number is 1-800-322-2000. If you find it difficult to get to a Waldenbooks' store to get the application for the Preferred Reader program, you can also get an application by calling this number.

WHEN BIGGER IS BETTER

Sometimes, large print editions can make reading more enjoyable for you or someone you care about. At least one publisher, Thorndike Press in Thorndike, Maine publishes a fantastic variety of large-print current best sellers, romances, biographies, non-fiction, westerns, adventure/suspense books, inspirational and other books to fascinate the most demanding reader. In early 1990, the titles they had available included Tom Clancy's *Clear and Present Danger*, Alice Walker's *The Temple of My Familiar*, Judith Viorst's *Forever Fifty and Other Negotiations*, and Andrew M. Greeley's *St. Valentine's Night.*

Thorndike's Reader's Guild offers members a 25 percent discount on the full cost of their books (which are very reasonably priced). There is no charge to join the Guild and you are not required to purchase a minimum number of books. If you prefer to use large print publications, you will be delighted that they have even printed their order forms and much of the catalog in large print. For more information, they maintain a toll-free telephone line for customers from the U.S. and Canada at 1-800-223-6121 except in Maine, where residents can call (207) 948-2963 collect.

GROCERY STORES

There are some major categories of retailers who do not normally offer discount programs for mature shoppers. Often, their reasons fall into two categories. Either their pricing structure already has such a tight profit margin that they have no leeway to make further discounts or the logistics are impossible. Luckily, many of them will still find a way to go that extra mile for you.

Grocery stores fall into the tight profit margin area. Many were contacted while this book was being researched. Those responding expressed a sincere desire to be able to serve their mature shoppers through discounts, but most reluctantly admitted that it simply was not possible. However, those with in-store pharmacies sometimes have a policy of offering discounts on prescription drugs (see Chapter 6).

There is at least one grocery store that does offer a cash discount. In the small town of Blue Ridge, Georgia, people age 65 or older can save 10 percent on their grocery purchases at Johnny's Food City on Wednesdays.

Owner Johnny Montgomery agrees that it is impossible to make money in the grocery business and offer senior discounts too.

But he offers discounts anyway.

He says, "When it comes to Wednesdays, I lose money. No question about it. I want to help the older people out. That's it in a nutshell."

Many of his customers cash their small Social Security checks at his store when they buy groceries, and seeing how little they have to live on, he feels strongly that it is important to help them.

Certainly, one of the reasons he can do this is because he is the owner of the store and does not have to answer to shareholders as many grocery chain managers do. However, in talking to Montgomery, it is apparent that his caring attitude is felt and appreciated throughout the community. In spite of losing money on Wednesdays, his business shows a profit which he shares with the employees.

Another grocery store chain has come up with a way of giving you a good deal that is not really a discount. It is more of a gift.

The Kroger stores in Ohio (except Dayton and Cincinnati) and part of West Virginia (near Wheeling), send special Golden Touches coupon books to members of Ohio's Golden Buckeye and West Virginia's Golden Mountaineer programs in their store areas.

Since this program began in 1989, members receive a special coupon book every six months. There is a coupon for each Tuesday (since Tuesdays are traditionally slow days). Each coupon could be for a free item, like a head of lettuce, or perhaps 50 cents off a more expensive item.

Kroger's spokesperson says that usually the vendors are an important part of the program since they donate to the effort and Kroger will often match their donation.

MAIL ORDER

Logistics come into play with mail order houses. How can they be sure they are giving the discounts just to mature Americans?

At Lillian Vernon, selling by mail-order catalog makes it impossible to accurately gauge the age of their customers for every order. Their spokesperson notes that many seniors are either too busy to shop or may have mobility problems relating to health, so catalog shopping is especially attractive to them.

At Lillian Vernon they have developed a special service which is available to everyone, but they find is especially appreciated by their mature customers. Their "Send A Gift" program enables their customers to have the gift they choose from the catalog shipped directly to the recipient — bypassing the need to re-box and re-ship it. This service costs $2 for each address you want items mailed to. On the outside of the box is a postage label that says it is a gift and who it is from.

AND THERE IS MORE

These programs give you an idea of the kinds of discounting programs offered by major retailers. You may be able to find other programs at retailers in your community by doing a little sleuthing. It never hurts to ask — and as you can see from these programs — it could *really* pay off in deals and discounts for you.

CHAPTER 4:
DISCOUNTS FROM
RESTAURANTS

"Can we ever have too much of a good thing?"
Cervantes, (1605) **Don Quixote de la Mancha**

Hungry right now? You will be before you finish reading this chapter.

Whether it is a quick hamburger with your grandchildren, a leisurely meal with good friends, or a romantic candlelight dinner for two, eating out is one of life's most pleasant pastimes.

Luckily for you, restaurants for every cuisine and in every price range want your business, and are willing to go out of their way to attract you.

One reason they are so eager for your business is because you are in an age group which is very likely to eat out. U.S. Department of Commerce figures for 1986 show that if you are between the ages of 45 and 54, you probably spend $27.47 every week for food away from home. From ages 55 to 64, the figure only goes down to $20.05. When you compare this with the $17.28 that young people under 25 spend, it is easy to see why your business is so attractive.

It would be wonderful if each national restaurant chain offered a consistent discount in all their restaurants. Then you could easily compare offers before deciding where to go. Unfortunately, it does not work that simply.

There are a few basic problems which complicate things, especially in fast food restaurants. First, there is frequently no system-wide program. Chains may franchise some stores and own others outright. The corporate office may define a discount plan and then leave it to the local managers or owners to implement if they choose. In other chains, the corporate offices simply leave the whole idea of whether to offer a discount and what it should be up to the local restaurant.

This can mean that you may be eligible for a significant discount at one restaurant, but at another restaurant in the next town, you may not receive any discount at all even though they are part of the same chain.

This corporate confusion can also make it somewhat difficult to find out if a chain offers a discount. One company contacted at the corporate level said they had no senior discounts. Yet, one of their regional offices said they did — and sent a copy of the card to prove it.

The programs which the restaurants offer can take many forms. Perhaps the most popular is the cash discount which may be expressed as either a flat amount or a percentage of the bill. For example, at participating Chi-Chi's Mexican Restaurants, customers can ask for the "Silver Dollar" card which entitles them to $1 discount off each $5 food purchase — effectively 20 percent off.

Some restaurants offer a premium such as a free beverage when you buy a meal. Burger King is one of these. They will give you a free cup of coffee or small soft drink with any purchase at a participating restaurant if you are at least 55. Jack in the Box makes the same offer, except you get to choose when you consider yourself a "mature" American.

Both of these (and many other) restaurants make the cards available in their restaurants. If you do not see any notices about them — ask.

Also, when you are on vacation, remember to ask for discounts. Some chains have inconsistent discount policies which may actually work in your favor when you are out of town.

Louis Trachtman, a retired accountant from Philadelphia, especially enjoys his Arby's discount — when he is on Atlantic City's famous Boardwalk.

He and his wife found out about this discount because it was posted in the store (a great customer service). Now when they go on their frequent trips to the ocean — and as Louis says, "make our contributions" to local casinos — they both use their Arby's discount cards to get 20 percent off their meal. Then they enjoy it from the restaurant as they sit and overlook the activity on the Boardwalk.

SENIOR MENUS — ARE THEY FOR YOU?

Still other restaurants offer a special Senior Menu. Before you order from a Senior Menu, you may want to check with your waiter to see if the servings on this special menu are the same as the same dinner ordered from the regular menu. A smaller serving may be perfect if you have a smaller appetite, but if you have worked up a really big appetite, a smaller serving may leave you still hungry.

A spokesperson for Denny's restaurants explains how their Senior Menu works. The entrée portion is usually half the size that it would be if ordered from the regular menu. Vegetable and side dish servings are the same as on the regular menu. The prices are anywhere from 25 to 35 percent less than the regular menu price. The response to having a special menu, lower prices and smaller portions has been very favorable and Denny's representatives say the Senior Menu is here to stay.

Lyons restaurants offer both a senior menu and a discount of 10 percent for customers age 60 or older. At Lyons, holders of their "Senior Privilege Card" card get the full 10 percent discount for everyone in the party if they pay the check. A spokesperson for Lyons notes that this policy makes it very attractive for their senior customers to bring the whole family in for a treat.

And then you get to the *really* good part. If you hold their Senior Privilege Card and choose your meal from their senior menu, you can actually take the ten percent discount off the senior menu price! How's that for a really good deal?

You also need to be aware that some restaurants have limits on the hours when they make these discount programs available. For instance, Sizzler Restaurants offer diners age 55 or over a 20 percent discount every day from 2 to 5 p.m. and all day Monday, Tuesday and Wednesday. Friendly's also limits discounts with its Friendly's Silver Service Club card to Monday through Friday and the hours of 1 to 6 p.m. Obviously, these are the times when the restaurants are less likely to be crowded. On the other hand, it is also a time when you are more likely to feel comfortable relaxing and dawdling over your meal.

When you are planning to use your senior discount at a restaurant, it is always a good idea to check first to see if this discount is the best available. Some restaurants offer special coupon discounts or "early bird" specials. Your discount may not be available on specials or with coupons and those offers may be better deals.

You should also check to see if the discount is available just to you. Many restaurants, like Carrows, will include all senior (from age 60) members of your party in their offer of 10 percent off all menu items, beverages and desserts to holders of their "Golden Card." However, like many other restaurant chains, the discount is not available on advertised television specials, table tents or other promotions. The Carrows spokesperson says this is because those items are already discounted in price.

ABOVE AND BEYOND

Then there are other restaurants which really get into the spirit of discounts and offer them in addition to their other promotional prices. For instance, at Papa Gino's of America, pizza and pasta lovers 60 and over can get 10 percent off their meal with a senior identification card. In addition, the discount can be used both with coupon promotions and on lunch and supper specials.

So far, the restaurants mentioned have been primarily fast food and family-style. However, many fancier establishments also will give discounts to mature customers. Some of these discounts may be available to you only if you belong to a specific seniors' organization which a restaurant may have made arrangements with. For instance, members of the Sears group, Mature Outlook, receive a 10 percent discount on food ordered in participating Holiday Inn Restaurants.

Some special benefit packages through hotels can also help you get a discount on fine dining. Hilton's H-Honors members are eligible for a 20 percent dinner discount for two at over 240 Hilton Restaurants in the U.S., regardless of whether you are staying at the hotel.

Often fine restaurants are independently owned. If you wonder whether a particular restaurant you are interested in offers a discount, call ahead. If you are told they do have special discount programs, be sure to get the name of the person who told you. Then, if there is confusion later at the restaurant, you know whom to ask for to clear it up.

You may also be able to find restaurants which offer special programs by looking through any of the small seniors' publications which are available in your area. Copies are often available free at libraries, senior centers and even grocery stores. Since their advertisers are local, they may include restaurant ads from area restaurants featuring different styles and cuisines.

RESOURCE ROUND-UP

Here are some of the restaurant chains which offer special deals and discounts for you. Because the discounts may vary in availability even within the same chain, always ask before you place your order.

If the restaurant requires identification, check with your local outlet to find out how to get their card. Contacting their corporate offices first may not be as efficient since some of the cards are issued on an outlet-by-outlet basis or through a regional program. Some restaurants also may only offer discounts to members of specific senior organizations.

RESTAURANT DEALS AND DISCOUNTS

Age	% Disc't	Sr. Menu	ID	Description
55	10-20%	yes	yes	ARBY'S - "Golden American Club" card, minimum age 55. Anywhere from 10 to 20 percent off your total bill depending on the store.
55	#1	#4	yes	BURGER KING - "Golden Years Guest Card." One card good in 49 states, must get separate card for Florida.
55	#2	#2	#2	CAPTAIN D'S SEAFOOD - Some offer a 10% discount, others may have a Seniors Menu.
60	10%	#4	yes	CARROWS or CARROWS CAFE & BAKERY - "Golden Card" also for take-out program where available.
62	20%	#4	yes	CHI-CHI'S - "Silver Dollar" card. $1 off each $5 food purchase.

55	#4	yes	no	DENNY'S
#2	#2	#2	#2	EL POLLO LOCO
55	15%	#4	yes	FRIENDLY'S - "Friendly's Silver Service" club card. Discount available Mon. - Fri. 1-6 p.m.
55	#2	#4	#2	HARDEE'S
50	10%	#4	yes	HOLIDAY INN - Your guest gets discount too.
60	20%	#4	yes	HILTON's HHONORS members
*	#1	#4	yes	JACK IN THE BOX - "Senior Save" card. *Minimum age: whenever you consider yourself a mature American.
#2	#2	#2	#2	KENTUCKY FRIED CHICKEN
55	#2	#2	#2	LEE'S FAMOUS RECIPE CHICKEN - Some offer a 10% discount. Others may offer a Senior Menu.
60	10%	yes	yes	LYON'S - "Senior Privilege Card" Discount covers whole party and can be applied to senior menu.
#4	#4	#4	#4	McDONALD'S - No company-wide program; local restaurants may design their own.
60	10%	#4	yes	PAPA GINO'S - Use any senior identification card. Discount

good even on specials.

60	10%	no	yes	QUINCY'S FAMILY STEAK-HOUSE
#2	#2	#4	#4	SADIE'S BUFFET & GRILL
55	#2	#2	#2	SHONEY'S - any senior identification card. Some restaurants offer a senior menu, others offer a cash discount.
55	20%	#4	yes	SIZZLER - "Senior Club" card, Restricted hours to Thurs-Sun. 2-5 p.m. and all day Mon-Wed
60	#2	#4	yes	WENDY'S - "Senior Citizen" discount card

Code List -

#1 Good for free coffee or small beverage with purchase
#2 Participating restaurants determine their own program
#3 Available to members of Mature Outlook (see Chapter
    11). Does not include alcoholic beverages, room service,
    tax or gratuity.
#4 Check with your local restaurant

CHAPTER 5:
DISCOUNTS FROM
SERVICE BUSINESSES

"You ain't heard nothin' yet, folks."
*Al Jolson in the first talking film, **The Jazz Singer**, 1927*

Service businesses are certainly the growth industry of the 1990s. Whether you are single or married, working or retired, it seems like there is never enough time or expertise to do everything for yourself.

Today you probably hire traditional service providers to handle many of your medical, legal and financial matters. You may also hire specialists in different fields when you get your hair cut, take your car in for an oil change, and need a gardener. In some communities, there are even hire service providers who will pick up your clothes at the dry cleaners, stand in line for you at the Department of Motor Vehicles and arrange a party for your grandchild.

Any firm which offers a service you are interested in may also be willing to offer you a discount to attract your business. Unlike major retailers who often (but not always) offer discounts because it is a good business strategy, many service providers will simply offer you a discount because they feel you deserve it. They may have seen mature customers whose situation was such that they needed the assistance and the business owners decided to offer it as a public service to all who had reached a certain age.

A BODY SHOP DOES NOT
DENT YOUR WALLET

In Hayward, California, Ray Souza, manager of Souza's Auto Body, offers people age 60 or older a 10 percent discount on their labor and parts.

In his community, he has seen many mature customers who found it difficult to pay for the deductible amount on their car insurance when they needed work done. Souza feels that these customers deserve any break they can get.

The discount he offers is figured on the labor and materials, and then applied to the deductible. This amount cannot exceed the person's insurance deductible because Souza believes that refunding money to the customer would be against the law.

However, the discount can make a significant difference for many people. If the customer needs $2,000 of work done and has a $250 deductible, the 10 percent discount of $200 means the customer only has to pay $50 out of his own pocket.

While Souza advertises his special discount, he says that some customers are still surprised to hear how it can help them. He has been offering this deal for several years and he finds that news of it has spread by work of mouth. He estimates that 25 percent of his customers are now taking advantage of this offer.

DON'T MISS AN OPPORTUNITY

Sometimes a service may seem so basic or so necessary that you may not even think of asking them for a discount. That could be a mistake that costs you money. When you call Roto-Rooter, you probably are not thinking about discounts — you are thinking about stopped-up drains. Roto-Rooter's spokesperson says that there is no corporate policy on discounts because the corporation is a mix of corporately owned and franchised locations.

He says they offer discounts in markets where it is a "competitive necessity." Sometimes the discount is mentioned in their advertising or their yellow pages listing in the phone book, but high advertising costs sometimes restrict the amount of information they can include in their ad. Since your local Roto-Rooter representative may offer a discount, it would certainly be worth your while to ask.

TAX PREPARATION

Unfortunately, one of the sure things in life is that you will have to pay taxes. Fortunately, you do not have to handle all the calculations by yourself.

H&R Block does not have a company-wide program of discounts for mature customers. However, many of their offices in the U.S. and Canada have created discounting programs designed specifically for people in their community.

Darrel Short, who has 28 H&R Block offices in Western Arkansas, says that he often offers a special discount to customers who are 55 or older. These customers receive 10 percent off their charges whether they have an inexpensive, simple return or a more expensive, complex return.

He says that his employees are also always on the look-out to help older people get the special tax breaks they may be entitled to because of age, etc.

H&R Block also offers a way some people can save money while they are learning how to make more. Some H&R Block offices offer a substantial discount for those who enroll in Block's Basic Income Tax Course. This 75-hour course will teach you the fundamentals of income tax preparation. It normally costs about $200 (costs vary regionally) and the savings for mature students can be as much as $50.

Depending on the needs of local H&R Block offices, you may be offered employment if you finish the course successfully (although there is no guarantee — and if employment is offered, taking the course does not obligate you to accept). You can also take the course in one place and work in another because if you accept employment, you will be taking a free 25-hour course which will teach you the new federal laws and the state and/or local laws in the area where you will be working.

LOOKING GOOD

The desire to look your best does not change as you mature. One part of looking good that you have paid for over and over again is hair cutting/styling. Many locally owned hair salons and barber shops have given discounts to their mature customers for many years.

In recent years, there has been a phenomenal growth of hair-cutting chains. At least two of them make discounts available especially to you.

At Pro-Cuts you only pay $4 for a haircut if you are 50 or older. They also offer shampoo and styling services.

You will find Fantastic Sam's throughout the U.S. and Canada. While the discounting programs they offer will vary from region to region, most areas have implemented the Fantastic Years Club which requires a membership card (ask about their policy at your local Fantastic Sam's). Some salons have set hours on certain days and offer mature customers anywhere from 20 percent to 50 percent of all services and products.

PICTURE PERFECT

Now that you look so great, how about having your picture taken?

Once you are 60 or older, Olan Mills Studios in the U.S. and Canada want to give you a 10 percent discount on all your purchases there. They can save you even more money by using their Club Plan (which is available to all customers). The Club Plan, which is sold by telemarketing, entitles the customer to three sittings, 90 days apart, and the customer receives a complimentary 8 x 10 inch custom natural portrait for each sitting.

Since many photographers are independent businesspersons, you may want to check with those in your area to see if they will give you a discount on your photography needs. Remember, the photos you have made now are a way of preserving precious memories and they will become treasured heirlooms in time to come.

MAID TO ORDER?

Certainly housecleaning is one area of service that many people use at some time in their life. According to "55 Plus: Volume II," which was written by S. Amanda Putnam and Carl E. Steidtmann and published by the Management Horizons division of Price Waterhouse, the use of regular maid services increases with age. They imply that the 55 Plus consumers are increasingly using their dollars to buy comfort and reduce physical stress.

In what may seem unusual, a survey of many companies offering maid services did not turn up any who offered discounts to their mature clients.

One spokesperson for a maid service reasoned that people who hire this type of service fall into two categories.

Some of them want the benefits that come with hiring an agency. They expect their house cleaners to be trained, bonded and insured. They believe this gives them some assurance that their home will be cleaned well and their property respected.

He says that others who hire household help are more interested in the bottom line — how economically can they hire some help. He notes that people whose primary orientation is toward the bottom line are more likely to hire someone privately. The agencies may not seem economically competitive to these people since the fees that agencies charge must reflect their overhead expenses as well as the direct costs for the employees who do the cleaning.

There is one way some people become eligible for housekeeping assistance. Some states have programs to help the frail elderly continue to live in their own homes. These programs will pay for some housekeeping services under certain conditions. If you or someone you care about has become too frail to handle his housekeeping, check with your state department of aging to see if there is a program in your area.

Unfortunately, housecleaning companies are not the only service businesses who do not offer age-specific discounts.

Some business owners believe that there is no reason for them to offer a discount because their business is not something they usually have a lot of repeat sales on. If you check, however, you may find they offer some discounts based on other factors. For instance, some people who offer color/fashion analysis services will give discounts if two or more people want their colors analyzed at the same time, because it is more efficient for them.

What can you do to help convince these service-based businesses to offer discounts? See if they offer also offer a product which leads to repeat sales (like makeup). If you can how them the potential for repeat sales, they may be more interested in offering a discount. In addition, consider asking for discounts if you can supply a number of customers at one time.

A BIRD IN THE HAND

The discounts and deals mentioned above can be exciting new ways to save money on services you need. At the same time, do not overlook the services available through groups you already belong to.

If you are a Y.E.S. member, you can save 20 percent on regular priced haircuts, permanents, hair coloring, manicures and pedicures at participating Montgomery Ward Hair Salons.

Other services Y.E.S. members can receive discounts

on include Ward's floral service, engraving service, and even on lessons at Arthur Murray Dance Studios. You can also save up to $4 per item on gift wrapping by using the special coupons in the Y.E.S. club magazine.

Any organization you belong to in your community which is oriented toward the needs of people your age has the potential for having a program which includes merchant and service discounts. This could be just a sports or retirement club, or it could be the chapter of a larger organization like the American Association of Retired Persons, the Canadian Association of Retired Persons and The Retired Officers Association.

Perhaps you belong to a senior membership program through your local hospital (these plans are discussed in detail in Chapter 6.) Some of these programs have tie-ins with the local business community and may have a list of service businesses which offer discounts to mature customers.

Check with your local senior center. Even if you are not currently interested in joining in the social activities there, they may be able to give you information about which local service providers will give you a discount.

Remember that service is the byword for the 1990s. Many businesses competing in the service marketplace will be eagerly vying for your patronage. So keep a look out for the ones which are willing to give you special deals and discounts to attract your business.

CHAPTER 6:
DISCOUNTS ON MEDICAL
SUPPLIES/SERVICES

*"A wise man should consider that health
is the greatest of human blessings,"*
Hippocrates (c. 460-400 b.c.)
Regimen in Health, bk IX

Medical stuff. Oh, no. Scary, confusing, expensive and depressing. Right?

Well, not exactly.

Actually, not by a long shot.

The good news is that there are all kinds of resources to help you get great deals and discount for all your health needs. Some offer education and information, some discounts on prescriptions and over the counter drugs, others have become multi-service programs with the most unexpected benefits.

Why are so many health care concerns competing for you business? Once again, it is a matter of economics. Figures from AARP and the Administration on Aging of the U.S. Department of Health and Human Services shows that people age 65 and over represented only 12 percent of the U.S. population in 1987, yet they accounted for 36 percent of the total personal health care expenditures.

This worked out to $5,360 per year for each older person versus only $1,290 for younger persons. If you were in this business, which customer would you set your cap for?

Even in the area of cosmetics and bath products, people age 50 and better make up about 26 percent of the U.S. population, yet you account for 37 percent of the purchases of those products. That is a lot of makeup, bubble bath and shaving cream!

SOMETHING FOR EVERYONE

To simplify this very complicated subject, this chapter is broken down into specific areas of interest, such as prescriptions, eye care, hearing aids, etc.

Several of the comprehensive plans which offer a variety of services are offered by department stores and are outlined in Chapter 3. Where a specific benefit is offered through membership in another group, it is noted here.

This is by no means a complete list of programs offered to help you save money on your health needs. Keep an eye out for special benefits through groups you already belong to and the possibility of acquiring new benefits by joining new groups or programs.

PRESCRIPTIONS

After a survey of the options available, it almost becomes unbelievable that anyone pays full price for prescription drugs. Certainly, when you need them, drugs prescribed by your physician can help you lead a longer, more comfortable and more productive life. And although you will have to pay something for the privilege (unless you have a superduper drug coverage included in your health insurance), there is no reason to pay more than you have to.

One caution. Whether you choose to use a neighborhood pharmacy or order medications by mail (or a little of both) you need be careful. In these days of using different medical specialists for each specific problem, it becomes especially important that your pharmacist be aware of all the medications you are taking (both prescription and over-the-counter). Only then can he or she warn you about any potential dangers by combining medications which you are using.

If you take medications regularly, it is a good idea for you to keep a list of your medications in your wallet. It should include the name of the drug (since names can sound similar), the exact dosage (when you do not feel good is no time to try to remember 5 milligrams or .5), the prescription number and the pharmacy where it is usually filled. Then if there is any question about the safety of mixing your new prescription with the old, the pharmacist filling your current prescription can check it out for you.

In all probability, your neighborhood pharmacy offers you a discount. These pharmacies can also be vital if you tend to have your prescription changed often, only need medication for temporary conditions (like antibiotics for infections), and tend to wait until the last minute to refill your prescriptions.

A pharmaceutical division of that old favorite, JC Penney Co., operates in 20 states and is known under two different names. In the South and Midwest, their approximately 125 stores are known as Treasury Drug. In other states they have approximately 350 Thrift Drug Stores.

The stores offer a 10 percent discount on prescriptions and selected over-the-counter merchandise to their patrons. You must be at least 60 years old to apply for their Senior Citizen Discount Card unless you live in New Jersey where the law requires you be 62.

According to the New Jersey Board of Pharmacy, all drug dispensers in the state must follow the regulations in the statutes governing the practice of pharmacy including N.J.S.A. 45:14-12f. This regulation prohibits them from giving premiums or rebates of any kind to persons under the age of 62.

All Payless Drug Stores in the nine western states are company owned, but according to their spokesperson, there is no company-wide discount program. He says that customers in the states of Oregon, Washington and Idaho are the most likely to find their store giving a discount on the prescriptions they fill for mature customers. However, that does not mean that their other stores are overcharging.

He explains that in many communities, especially in California, the competition for business is so strong that the prices in those stores must be kept at rock bottom to stay competitive in the marketplace. He cautions consumers to not get caught up in choosing their pharmacy only on the basis of which ones give discounts, since the thing that really matters is the net cost you pay.

GOOD DEALS, BUT NOT NECESSARILY CASH

At Osco Drugs and Savon Drugs the corporate policy does not include a specific discount program for mature customers (although it could not hurt to ask if your neighborhood store offers a program). That does not mean they are not trying to do things to attract you and make you feel that shopping there gives you a good deal.

Their spokesperson states that of special interest to their 'over 50' customers is the Osco/Savon "For Your Good Health," publication which is available in their stores. This booklet is filled with health care information and includes valuable coupons with up to six months in redemption value.

At Fay's Drugs 185 stores in New York and Pennsylvania, they start with a basic 10 percent discount on prescriptions and store brand merchandise. Then they add extra benefits like their quarterly newspaper and coupon book which their "Senior Saver" program members receive by mail. In addition, they do health screenings to help their customers take care of themselves.

ENOUGH WITH THE OTHER BENEFITS, BACK TO THE $

At over 2,000 Revco Discount Drug stores in 28 states, customers age 60 or over and those who will turn 60 during that calendar year can get 10 percent off the regular price of prescriptions and Revco brand products like toiletries, etc. every day. All they need is the Revco Senior Citizen's discount card which can be applied for in any store. In June of 1988, Revco decided to expand their program even more and now they offer a bonus day.

On Wednesdays, shoppers who have the Revco Senior Citizen's discount card can expand their 10 percent discount to nearly everything in the store. The only things excluded from this offer are beverages, tobacco products and third party prescriptions. At the time Revco announced the expanded discount program, their Executive Vice President Carl Bellini recognized your economic power in the marketplace when he said, "We want Revco to remain a leading health care provider to our senior citizens. While we recognize that non-prescription, over-the-counter health care purchases for senior citizens differ significantly from those under 55, their economic power is compelling."

SAVE TIME WHILE YOU SAVE MONEY

Not only free-standing drug stores will give you discounts. Many grocery stores now include a pharmacy department where customers can have their prescriptions filled while they shop.

At Pathmark Supermarkets in New Jersey, New York, Pennsylvania, Connecticut and Delaware, they offer a 10 percent discount on prescription drug purchases made in the store.

The discount on prescriptions is normally only good on purchases you make for yourself. A prescription for a third party, such as a family member or friend, will usully cost full price.

Here is a list of some of the places where you can receive a discount on your prescription needs. Some of them may also offer discounts on their house brand products. Check with the pharmacy clerk at your neighborhood store to see if there are any other special benefits at their particular store.

DRUG STORE DEALS AND DISCOUNTS

Age	Disc't	I.D.Card	Other	Company
60	10%	yes	#1	FAY'S DRUGS: NY & PA
60	15%	yes	#1	HARCO DRUGS: AL, FL & MS
60	10%	yes	#5	K & B Inc.: LA, MS, AL, FL, TX
60	10%	no	#5	KERR DRUG STORES, INC.: NC & SC
60	10%	no	#2	LUCKYS: CA, NV
#4	#4	#4	#4	OSCO/SAVON DRUGS
#5	10%	#5	#2	PATHMARK
#5	#5	#5	#3	PAYLESS: 9 Western States
60	10%	yes	#1	REVCO: 28 States
60	10%	#5	#1	THRIFT DRUG/TREASURY DRUG STORES (Subsidiary of JC Penney)

Code List -

#1 Also available on store brand products

#2 Available in grocery stores with full-service, in-house pharmacies

#3 Individual stores set their own policy

#4 No discount on national basis, but individual stores may have special programs or premiums

#5 Check at your local store

MAIL ORDER PHARMACIES

Ordering prescription medication by mail offers you several benefits. Perhaps the most compelling is that you do not have to wait in line with people who may have contagious illnesses.

In addition, there is the convenience factor. Your orders are delivered to your door. This is especially helpful if you have a physical disability which makes it difficult to get out — or a tremendously active lifestyle, and you think waiting in line is a waste of your time.

According to the companies which offer mail order convenience, you may also find that you are saving a substantial amount of the money it would cost you to have your prescription filled locally. Working from large, centralized facilities gives them the economy of doing business for a large number of people that numerous, small, local pharmacies serving the same number of people simply can not match.

Some mail order prescription firms require that you be a member of a specific organization like AARP to use their services. Others, like American Pharmacy Service (APS), have you join either as a member of a group or as an individual (for $49 for a single member or $75 for a family membership).

Before you use any mail-order pharmacy, be sure to check their costs for your prescriptions. Each company advertises that they offer great prices, but the prices on the specific drugs you need may be higher at one pharmacy than another.

AARP has been offering their Pharmacy Service since 1959 because back even then, the organization saw prescription prices rising quickly. If you are an AARP member, you can order both prescription and over-the-counter items through a regional service center.

They offer colorful, seasonal catalogs where you can order anything from antacids and shampoos to vitamins, razor blades to hearing aid batteries. Some of the items carry the AARP Pharmacy Service label and cost even less than the discounted national brands of those types of products.

For example, in their Winter 1990 catalog, you could have purchased 300 Bayer Aspirin for $8.69. At the same time, you could have bought 500 of their house brand 'light coated aspirin' for $2.94.

Your prescriptions can be transferred to their pharmacy either by phone or by mail. AARP Pharmacy Service will even have the medication labels printed in Braille if you ask. They have toll-free customer service lines which are available to members so that people can check the prices of any drugs they are interested in.

American Pharmacy Service (APS) (1-800-346-2156, in Indiana call 1-219-736-7600) recognizes people can find the whole idea of needing to take medicines depressing, so they have taken steps to at least make it a pleasure to receive your medications. When you order from APS, the first thing you are likely to notice is the shiny, colorful "happy face" sticker on the outside, thanking you for your business. Inside, along with your medications (and statement, of course), you may find a cheerful saying from your personal pharmacist and a free sample of some toiletry that he or she thought you might enjoy trying.

Another thing to check when you are pricing mail-order pharmacies, is how much the shipping and handling or mailing costs will add to the final price you will have to pay. Some, including Medi-Mail, Inc. (1-800-331-1458) have no additional charge for those services.

Like many of these other mail-order pharmacies, Medi-Mail has many membership groups like the National Association for Retired Credit Union People, American Federation of Police and Hadassah who subscribe to their service.

If you belong to an affinity group, there may be a mail-order pharmacy that they already work with. If not, consider bringing up this kind of affiliation to your organization.

Some mail-order pharmacies will also serve people who are not members of any group, but who call up and ask. Call the toll-free numbers noted in this chapter to get the specifics.

For instance, Family Pharmaceuticals (1-800-922-3444) says that while they are known by many people because of the affinity groups and insurance companies they work with, their services are available to everyone.

To get started, you would call them, get a quote, and send in your prescription along with a check for the cost of filling that prescription. They will also be glad to send you a catalog. As an added benefit to those who do not belong to an organization they do business with, Family Pharmaceuticals charges everyone the same price, so there is no extra cost to do business with them as an individual.

Again, since each person's medical needs are unique, you should check the prices of the medications you use at several neighborhood and mail-order pharmacies before you decide which offers you the best prices and services for your situation.

OPTICAL

Your vision is a precious resource that is well worth taking care of. Fortunately, there are some wonderful programs which offer you free or discounted examinations and discounts on the services and products you need to help you see your best.

There are Optical Departments in many Sears Stores nationwide and there are two ways you can save here. Members of Sears' Mature Outlook (see chapter 11), are eligible for a 20 percent discount on regular prices of frames, prescription lenses and contact lenses at participating locations. Mature Outlook members are also eligible for a discount of over 40 percent on Sears' Vision One program.

Vision One members can save up to 50 percent on eyewear products at participating locations of the Optical Department at Sears. When you make your purchase, you just show the card — no forms to fill in. Your membership card also provides full coverage for your immediate family (spouse and/or children living at home).

At Montgomery Ward, you have the opportunity to save 20 percent on prescription lenses, frames and (where permitted by state law) contact lenses. You can use this offer on all types of eyewear, including bifocals, trifocals, no-line bifocals, prescription sunglasses, sports and designer frames, soft and hard contact lenses.

There is a fairly new (1987) program called Opticare 2000 which may be available to you. It is currently offered as a benefit through some affinity groups including the Association of Retired Americans and the National Association of Retired Federal Employees. If you are not a member of any group they work with, you can still get these benefits by calling their phone number listed below. They will then refer you to your local program director.

Opticare is a national program which serves the optical needs of mature Americans. It works to address the special needs people in this age group have, including out-of-pocket expenses, insurance processing and education.

The benefits you would become eligible for as an Opticare member include: free vision screenings for cataracts, glaucoma and visual acuity; discounts on eyeglasses; free minor eyeglass adjustments; referral services; emergency service; Medicare assignment and insurance counseling and processing and free round-trip transportation from the sponsoring organization (i.e. senior center, service club, etc.) for scheduled eye exams and surgical care.

This is quite a deal since all these services are available at no cost to you. The expenses of the organization are underwritten by their co-sponsoring professionals who are ophthalmologists, optometrists, and opticians.

For more information call them at 1-800-628-5665.

HEARING AIDS

Sometimes it is possible to lose a significant amount of your hearing before you are even sure something is wrong. All kinds of factors, including loud noises in work or recreational activities can contribute to a reduction in hearing acuity.

Fortunately, there is a wide variety of hearing aids to make it possible for you to regain your ability to hear your grandchildren's laugh, birds in your garden, and other precious sounds.

There is also a variety of programs, including those below, to help you afford the assistance that can help you hear those special sounds.

At larger Montgomery Ward stores, their Y.E.S. members can receive an automatic $50 reduction on the price of one hearing aid or $100 on two regularly priced hearing aids. Members can get an identical benefit as a refund if they purchase their hearing aid through Beltone Hearing Centers.

Like the mail-order pharmacies, even hearing aid suppliers can keep their prices down when they do business from centralized locations. Association Hearing Service in Boulder, Colorado (1-800-333-HEAR) offers name brand hearing aids at about half the price these same aids would cost you at a local provider. Prices in a recent catalog ranged from $249 to $399.

They suggest that you have an audiogram done by an audiologist, physician or professional at a hearing and speech clinic and then mail the results to them. If that is not possible, they ask for a detailed letter outlining how your hearing loss affects you in different situations.

When you order, you need to enclose a refundable deposit of $100 unless you are a member of a group or policy holder of an insurance company which deals with Association. If you are, the aid or aids will be sent on approval.

With the newspapers full of stories about swindlers and cheats, sending valuable merchandise out with a small or no deposit might seem foolhardy, but not to the Association Hearing Service President Richard Wallace.

He says, "We are rarely taken advantage of. Most of the people we deal with are older and almost without exception, honest. We have sent eight or nine aids to someone and they either love or hate them, and then they either pay for them or return them." He adds that they only lose about six aids a year. His suspicion is that most of those are lost in the confusion when the customer dies during the 30-day free trial period.

SURPRISE BENEFITS

As you probably already suspect, providers of medical supplies and services see you and your peers as an inevitably-growing market. They really want to make you happy so that you will use, and be loyal to, their services.

Some hospitals have programs which are designed to garner your good will and loyalty so that you will turn to them for your health needs. The American Hospital Association says that these programs may have different names, but most offer the same basic services.

These services usually include monthly newsletters, health screenings for problems like high blood pressure, breast cancer or osteoporosis as well as help filling out Medicare, physician and supplemental insurance forms. Some programs include free or discounted health and fitness programs, discounts at the hospital pharmacy, vision center, cafeteria and gift shop.

The MuirCare program at John Muir Hospital in Walnut Creek, California is one of those programs. Membership is free to people who have Medicare and supplemental insurance. That normally means you would need Medicare A which is the hospital insurance everyone is entitled to as well as Medicare B. B covers out-patient services, etc. and people can elect to pay for it out of their Social Security check. A supplemental health insurance plan is also required unless you have a household income of less than $15,000.

The benefits are as varied as they are interesting. Of course, they offer health screenings, educational seminars, and a newsletter. They also offer to bill Medicare and your supplemental insurance for all inpatient and outpatient services provided at their facility. There are discounts on meals in the hospital dining room and on an emergency call button you can wear for safety and independence. Members are eligible for a special registration procedure to assist them if they need to check into this hospital.

In what might seem a little unusual for a hospital-based plan, MuirCare 65 also offers its members discounts at participating local merchants. Some, like shops which make eyeglasses, have a medical tie-in. Others, like beauty salons and art galleries, are included to add to the members' quality of life.

FREEBIES — FREEBIES — FREEBIES

The National Institute on Aging has gathered a tremendous amount of information which you can use to help you with your health concerns. These information-packed resources are available by mailing your request to:

> National Institute on Aging Information Center
> P.O. Box 8057
> Gaithersburg, MD 20898-8057

Single copies are free, and when inventory permits, they will fill bulk orders. Since the material is not copyrighted, you can also feel free to copy any information you want and republish it in your organization's newsletters or other places where you can use it to help others.

Here are some of the titles of publications available in 1990:

- *Resource Directory for Older People*
- *What is Your Aging IQ?*
- *Accidental Hypothermia: A Winter Hazard for Older People*
- *Accidental Hyperthermia: A Hot Weather Hazard for Older People*
- *Exercise Packet*
- *Health Resources for Older Women*
- *Nutrition Packet*
- *The Menopause Time of Life*
- *Women's Age Page Packet*

The NIA also publishes their Age Pages to provide a quick, practical look at some of the health topics that interest mature people. Selected titles are available in Chinese (C) or Spanish (S). If they all look interesting, you can simply order the complete set either bound or unbound.

Diseases/Disorders

- *AIDS and Older Adults*
- *Arthritis Advice* (C)
- *Cancer Facts for People Over 50* (C)
- *Dealing With Diabetes* (C) (S)
- *High Blood Pressure: A Common But Controllable Disorder* (C)
- *Osteoporosis: The Bone Thinner*
- *Senility: Myth or Madness?*
- *Stroke Prevention* (S)
- *Urinary Incontinence*
- *What to do About Flu* (C)

Health Promotion

- *Aging and Alcohol Abuse*
- *Can Life Be Extended?*
- *Don't Take it Easy*
- *Exercise!*
- *Smoking: It's Never Too Late To Stop*

Medical Care

- *Considering Surgery?*
- *Finding Good Medical Care for Older Americans*
- *When You Need a Nursing Home*

- *Who's Who in Health Care* (S)

Medications
- *Safe Use of Medicines by Older People* (C)
- *Safe Use of Tranquilizers*
- *"Shots" for Safety*
- *Should You Take Estrogen?*

Nutrition
- *Be Sensible About Salt*
- *Dietary Supplements: More is Not Always Better* (C)
- *Hints for Shopping, Cooking, and Enjoying Meals*
- *Nutrition: A Lifelong Concern* (C) (S)

Safety
- *Accidents and the Elderly* (S)
- *Crime and the Elderly* (S)
- *Health Quackery - Heat, Cold, and Being Old* (S)
- *Preventing Falls and Fractures*
- *Safety Belt Sense*

Your Aging Body
- *A Good Night's Sleep*
- *Aging and Your Eyes*
- *Constipation* (C)
- *Digestive Do's and Don'ts* (S)
- *Food Care for Older People* (C)(S)
- *Hearing and the Elderly*
- *Prostate Problems*

- *Sexuality in Later Life*
- *Skin Care and Aging* (S)
- *Taking Care of Your Teeth and Mouth*

Other Titles

- *Getting Your Affairs in Order*

At the time you read this, some of these titles may no longer be available and there may be new titles which would address your concerns. When you send in your order, be sure to ask for a current publication list to be sure you have all the up-to-date information.

CHAPTER 7: DISCOUNTS FROM INSURANCE COMPANIES

> *"A penny saved is a penny gained."*
> *Thomas Fuller,* **Worthies** *1662*

Can you save money on your insurance needs? Probably more than you think. One way you can save is through discounts on your auto insurance. More on that later.

The main way to save money on your insurance is to buy smart. Any time you are in a life-stage involving change, you need to reevaluate your insurance needs. You may need more of one kind and less of another.

With all the different insurance products and all the claims they make, it can be hard to sort out what kinds and amount of insurance you really need. As a consumer, the ultimate responsibility for choosing good insurance coverage falls on your shoulders. No insurance is a good deal if it duplicates coverage you already have.

For instance, most health policies are written so that the accumulated total of all payments for covered health care billings will not be more than 100 percent of the charges — no matter how many policies you have. And yes, they do talk to each other.

National Association of Life Underwriters' spokesperson Patty Briotta also advises consumers to be cautious about dread disease policies which only cover one possible problem like cancer or Alzheimer's disease. She tells consumers to first get a good, comprehensive policy which covers all conditions, since no one knows with certainty which disease they might get.

If you do that and still want a "dread disease" policy, remember that 100 percent maximum payment. You will not become rich by getting Alzheimer's.

About the only time that you can have benefits in excess of your actual expenses is when you have a hospital indemnity policy. These policies pay benefits only when you are hospitalized. The benefits are cash which you can use to pay any out-of-pocket expenses that arise. These policies are not considered duplicative by state insurance regulators.

A REALLY "GREAT DEAL"

One really good (and free) deal that you may want to take advantage of is the Senior Citizens Health Insurance Counseling (SCHIC) service which is offered by members of the National Association of Life Underwriters.

This service is offered either through seminars or individual meetings. It gives you professional assistance in evaluating your current insurance policies, your current and potential needs, and what kinds of insurance products might help you meet those needs. This service specially targets your Medicare and Medigap insurance. The counselors are active or retired professional underwriters and are trained to help you evaluate all your personal insurance needs.

These counseling meetings are completely objective

and are only informational. You may want to bring along an adult child so they will also know about your insurance coverage and will be better prepared to help you if the need arises. This program has been so well received because the counselors offer objective advice and never endorse any one company or product.

Sometimes people discover gaps or problems with their coverage and they want to meet with a professional underwriter (insurance agent) to correct the situation.

According the SCHIC guidelines, your counselor can give you a list of local life underwriters who can help you, but his or her name will not appear on the list. This guarantees you that the counselor is not using your session as a sales tool, and keeps their members to the highest ethical standards.

The SCHIC sessions are arranged through your local Life Underwriters' Association. Many times they are offered at Senior Centers or other places where groups of mature people meet. If you can not find a Life Underwriters' Association in your area, write to them at the address below and ask for the address of a nearby group:

National Association of Life Underwriters
1922 F Street, N.W.
Washington, DC 20006-4387

At press time, SCHIC programs were in place in over 20 states and were expanding to others. If it turns out that you are not in an area where the program is offered you have four options.

    1. You write — and have your friends write — to the NALU. Certainly a proven demand

for the service will help them establish it in your area.

2. Talk with your personal insurance agent or call your local Life Underwriters Association and encourage them to offer this service.

3. Contact your state department of insurance. Some states offer consumer counseling services.

4. Read some of the publications the NALU publishes which can help you understand your changing insurance needs. You can get one copy of any or all of the pamphlets listed below by sending the NALU (address above) your request along with a stamped business size #10 envelope addressed to you. For fastest service, be sure to include the code number before each pamphlet with your request.

- DD1 *Points To Ponder If You're Considering Replacing Your Life Insurance*. This covers the benefits and risks of replacing your current life insurance policy with something new. It talks about accumulated vs. future cash values, contestable periods, etc.

- DD2 *Life Insurance, Choosing Your Best Buy*. Gives you definitions of the kinds of insurance, (whole life, universal life, variable life, etc.) and tips on how to pick an agent.

- DD3 *Long-Term Care Insurance*. Corrects common misconceptions and explains this new trend in insurance coverage.

LONG TERM CARE INSURANCE — YOUR HEALTH COMES FIRST

Probably no hotter topic exists for mature consumers considering their insurance needs than long term care insurance. No one wants to believe they will need it, but on the other hand, no one wants to risk becoming destitute before the governmental programs will kick in and help.

According to the (HIAA) Health Insurance Association of America, studies by the U.S. Department of Health and Human Services and the Brookings Institute indicate that persons aged 65 or more face a 40 percent chance of entering a nursing home for any length of time. For those who do, nearly 45 percent of them will stay three months or less.

Many people think that Medicare insurance will cover the cost of long-term care, such as care in a nursing home. Unfortunately, it only covers this care in certain cases. Your Medigap type insurance probably does not cover it either.

Until recently, most people have had to pay for their care with their own resources, or become impoverished in the process to qualify for Medicaid. A long-term care insurance policy can be a great "Deal" if it prevents you and your spouse from being forced to use most of your assets to pay for this care.

This is not a nickel and dime situation. Recent figures show that a year in a nursing home costs an average of $25,000. Higher in many areas. Home-based care provided by an aide just three times a week can run $440 per month. Skilled nursing assistance for those same three visits per week can easily add up to $8,200 per year.

While you are younger and healthier, it is easier to buy this kind of insurance. The amount of coverage you get will depend on several factors, including the company you choose and the amount of premium you can afford. There can be some limits and exclusions you need to be aware of when you choose a policy.

Following is a checklist to help you compare policies you may be considering. If you have other questions that are not asked here, be sure to ask them of each of the agents you are talking to.

LONG-TERM CARE POLICY CHECKLIST

Questions	Policy A	Policy B
1. What services are covered?		
• Skilled care		
• Intermediate care		
• Custodial care		
• Home health care		
• Adult day care		
• Other care		
2. How much does the policy pay per day for:		
• Skilled care		
• Intermediate care		
• Custodial care		
• Home health care		
• Adult day care		
• Other care		

3. Does the policy offer an inflation adjustment feature? If so, how does it work?

4. Does the policy have a maximum lifetime benefit? If so, what is it?
   - Nursing home
   - Home health

5. Does the policy have a maximum length of coverage per "spell of illness?" If so, what is it?
   - Nursing home
   - Home health

6. How long do I have to wait before preexisting conditions are covered?

7. Is Alzheimer's disease covered?

8. How many days is the elimination or deductible period before benefits begin?

9. Does this policy require:
   - Physician certification of need
   - A functional assessment
   - A prior hospital stay for:
     - Nursing home care
     - Home health care
   - A prior nursing home stay for home health care
   - Other

10. Can the policy be cancelled?

11. Will the policy cover me if I move to another area?

12. What is the age range for enrollment?

13. What does the policy cost?
- Per month
  - With inflation feature
  - Without inflation feature
- Per year
  - With inflation feature
  - Without inflation feature

Chart adapted from *Consumer's Guide to Long-Term Care Insurance.* Used with the permission of the Health Insurance Association of America.

MEDICARE SUPPLEMENT MAZE

One mistake that some consumers make is thinking that Medicare supplement insurance is the same as long-term care insurance.

It's not.

According to the Health Insurance Association of America, Medicare was never intended to cover all your health insurance needs. It was designed mainly to relieve people age 65 and older of part of the costs associated with hospitalization, surgery, home health care and skilled nursing care. Coverage has been extended to certain individuals under age 65 who are disabled or suffer from end-stage renal disease. After age 65, all persons eligible for Social Security also become eligible for Medicare whether they retire or choose to continue working.

As you may know, Medicare is divided into two parts.

Part A is a hospital insurance program. It is available without charge to everyone who is automatically eligible for it. People who are not automatically eligible must pay a monthly premium. To find out if your are eligible, check with your local Social Security office.

Medicare Part B is medical insurance to pay for physician and surgeon charges in and out of a hospital and for certain medical supplies. Part B is optional, and you can enroll if you are automatically eligible for Part A. There is a monthly premium for this coverage.

For more specific information about your eligibility and costs, you can obtain a copy of *Your Medicare Handbook* at your Social Security office. Since Social Security benefits and costs are always subject to change by the federal government, their office is the best place for you to get up-to-date information.

WHY SUPPLEMENT MEDICARE?

The reason many people choose to buy supplemental health insurance policies is that Medicare does not cover everything. There are restrictions on the length of time they will cover important benefits like skilled nursing care and home health care. Even for the care they do cover, you are responsible for the copayments and deductible amounts, which can add up quickly.

If you are age 65 or older and continue to work for an employer with 20 or more employees, your employer's health plan will pay your health bills with Medicare as a backup.

If you can not continue your group coverage, there are three basic kinds of individual insurance plans you can buy — although other forms of limited coverage are available. These are a medical expense policy, a hospital indemnity policy and a Medicare supplement policy.

Each policy has its benefits and drawbacks. Whichever type you choose, make your decision carefully. Investigate the benefits, weigh them against your other insurance policies and personal financial situation, and ask questions. If the agent or company will not explain it in a way you can understand, ask again until they do. If all else fails, contact your state department of insurance for help.

The Health Insurance Association of America offers *Deals & Discounts* readers two valuable booklets to help you understand the confusing language of insurance and answer commonly asked questions.

You can get *Long-Term Care Insurance* and/or *Medicare Supplement Insurance* free. Just write to them at:

Health Insurance Association of America
Fulfillment
P.O. Box 41455
Washington, DC 20018

AUTOMOBILE INSURANCE

As promised in the beginning of the chapter, there are some great deals and discounts available to you on your automobile insurance rates. These discounts are provided in recognition of the better experience realized by the group of individuals in the mature driver age range according to United States Fidelity and

Guaranty Company (USF&G Insurance). They start offering you a discount on your automobile operator's insurance as early as age 50.

Since individual states regulate the insurance industry within their borders, it is difficult to compare discounts. However, there are some factors that these discounts have in common.

One factor which can really help you access available discounts is to successfully complete a state-approved defensive driver or accident prevention course. Your personal auto insurance agent or local department of motor vehicles should be able to refer you to an approved course in your area.

Sometimes a group you belong to may offer this kind of approved course. According to AARP, their 55 Alive/Mature Driving course is the oldest and largest driver retraining program designed specifically for older motorists.

This comprehensive classroom course teaches participants about driving hazards, the effects of medications, local driving conditions, etc. Many insurance companies offer special discounts to graduates — and some states mandate that the insurance companies offer discounts to graduates.

Aetna Life & Casualty notes that the discounts for successfully completing these courses varies from five to ten percent depending on the state — and that different state have different age requirements which can vary from 55 to 82.

At the same time, Aetna offers its policyholders ages 55 through 64 a 10 percent discount on their auto premium, and policyholders age 65 and older receive a 20 percent discount.

The Nationwide Insurance companies also offer the same kinds of discounts, with exact benefits tied to the individual regulations in every state. For their basic mature driver discount, your driver's license may be all the identification you need. However, for the defensive driver discount, you will need to be able to show your certificate of completion to the agent. As a money-saving tip for your younger family members, Nationwide notes that in some states, all drivers who complete a defensive driver course are eligible for a discount on their premiums.

Check with different insurance companies which do business in your state to see exactly what the discount applies to. In the case of State Farm Mutual Automobile Insurance Company, the insurance rates are reduced 10 percent for liability, medical payments, personal injury protection, collision, and comprehensive coverage.

There may also be some restrictions which you did not expect. At State Farm, you are not eligible for the discount if you have a driver under the age of 25 living in your household.

If being able to renew your insurance throughout your lifetime concerns you, you will need to check with agents you are talking with to see if they guarantee to renew your policy.

If you have been a customer of the Safeco Insurance Companies for at least three years, they will guarantee to renew your insurance under certain conditions. To get this guarantee, all drivers in your family must be 50 or older, have no "gross" moving violations (such as driving under the influence), and you must have a history of paying your premiums on time.

Because the policy benefits and conditions can differ from state to state, your best bet for finding a good deal is to contact agents who work locally. You should be able to find them listed in your phone book.

When you are looking for a new agent, you should get recommendations from people whose judgment you respect. Then interview the candidates carefully. Ask them:

- Are they full-time agents who are committed to serving their clients needs, or is this something they do on the side?

- Do they belong to any professional organizations?

- Have they earned any professional designations like Chartered Life Underwriter (CLU)?

- Can they give you the names of their insurance clients who would recommend them?

GROUP RATES MEAN EXTRA SAVINGS

As you are checking around for the best deal on your insurance needs, remember to check out the different kinds of group insurance available to you through the organizations you belong to.

Some groups like AARP offer a wide range of group insurance opportunities like health insurance, homeowners insurance and automobile insurance. Another group, NARCUP, offers accidental death and dismemberment, senior life insurance, Medicare supplement, etc. They even offer a special life insurance plan you can purchase to protect your grandchildren.

For a look at what kinds of group insurance are available through some organizations you may belong to, see Chapter 11. Also, keep you eyes open for other group plans through other organizations you may belong to.

CHAPTER 8: PROMOTIONAL FARES FOR TRAVEL, HOTELS & AUTO RENTALS

"The use of traveling is to regulate imagination
by reality and instead of thinking how
things may be, to see them as they are."
From Mrs. Piozzi, *Anecdotes of Samuel Johnson (1786)*

Once upon a time, mature travelers could be counted on to do most of their traveling to see grandchildren or follow the winter sun. Today, you are just as likely to be taking a bicycle trip through California's Wine Country or traveling to poor countries to help the people there build schools and homes.

As a matter of fact, nearly 70 percent of you and your peers took a vacation in the last year and/or plan to take one in the next year.

Service and product providers have begun to recognize that once people hit their 50s and gain maturity, their travel is often motivated by their desire to live life to its fullest. Whether you want to experience novelty, personal growth or do things for others, your travel goals are likely to be highly individualized and oriented toward intangibles.

It comes as no surprise that the travel industry has also noticed that you travel — a lot. Figures show that people age 55 and over now buy 80 percent of the luxury travel, making your business especially attractive to travel service and product providers.

Whatever your reason for travel, this is one area where careful attention to discounting programs can yield major savings for you.

Since there is an incredible variety of discounts and programs to choose from, this chapter can only be a starting point for you. Rates and programs change rapidly in the travel industry so you will need to check with your travel agent or directly with the hotel, car rental, or other business to be sure you are getting the best possible rate.

Keep in mind that if you are able to plan ahead, travel at off-peak periods may enable you to save the most money.

HOTELS/MOTELS

Hotels and motels offer you a mind-boggling array of special discount programs. Some are run by the hotel chain itself, and others are programs offered through affinity groups like AARP.

In reading the following synopses of different hotel programs, remember that some hotels in any given chain may not be participating in the discount program or may have modified it to meet marketing conditions in their area. You may find that individual programs have some restrictions which could affect your plans.

Always check on the current conditions and availability of the money-saving programs before you make your reservations — and let them know you want the discount. If you wait until you are checking out, many chains will not honor your request for the discount. (Do not let these cautions intimidate you. The restrictions are usually common-sense things, and the benefits can be substantial.)

Also, this listing is a good starting point, but it does not cover every hotel chain or every discount program. So when you are considering travel, especially to major destinations, it will pay for you to compare prices and discounts that are offered by several hotels before making your decision.

IT ALL ADDS UP

To save you even more money, some chains offer a discount on meals in their restaurants, gift shops, etc. When you add these discounts together, the total amount of money you save can be substantial, so keep them in mind.

You may also find a convenience factor in using some of these programs since many keep records of your preferences for room size, (non)smoking, and ground or upper level.

Here, in alphabetical order, is an overview of some of the programs you can expect to find.

Days Inns, Hotels, Suites and DayStops   Since you are at least 50, you are eligible for membership in Days' "September Days Club." As a member, you (and your spouse sharing the same room) will receive discounts of between 15 and 40 percent on rooms, efficiency units and multi-room suites at participating Days.

You can save money with the 10 percent discounts

on meals at participating Days restaurants and purchases at participating Days gift shops.

Like many business-based clubs which are competing for your business, September Days members will find they receive some extra goodies. One which is typical is the club magazine. In this case, it is a quarterly, photographic travel magazine.

Other benefits include club-sponsored Travel Accident, Accidental Death and Dismemberment, Group Term Life, and Cancer Protector Plan insurance programs. For your health needs, the Club offers participation in Family Pharmaceuticals of America, Inc. which has discounts of up to 25 percent on prescribed brand-name medications and up to 50 percent on prescribed and over-the-counter generic medications, vitamins and other health aids.

In terms of extra travel benefits, you can save money through the Club on group and individual tours, car rentals through Alamo, and discounts of up to 50 percent at many theme parks, museums, and attractions.

Membership in the September Days Club costs $12 for one year with discounts if you sign up for more than one year ($27 for three years membership). For more information, call 1-800-241-5050.

Doral Hotels and Resorts Have you ever dreamed of "doing" New York? Doral Hotels and Resorts offer you the opportunity to do it first class if you are age 60 or older and are a member of their Doral Classics Club. The Doral Classics Club Concierge can assist you with your entertainment requests and reservations. You can even call ahead and make arrangements for your special trip.

They can help you get discounts at places you never thought you would have a chance to see. How about almost half off at the Guggenheim Museum or the Jewish Museum and half off at the Frick Collection and the Museum of Broadcasting?

New York has something for everyone, and the concierge at the Doral Hotels can help you find the places that will expand your world.

For more information, talk to your travel agent or call Doral Hotels & Resorts at (800) 223-5823.

Hampton Inn   With their LifeStyle 50 program, you can enjoy a tremendous discount on lodging costs when you travel with your spouse or friends. Membership entitles you to have up to three other adults stay in your room with you (provided no extra bedding is required), and only be charged the one-person rate each day for the room type you have chosen.

There is no cost for this program. Applications can be found at Hampton Inns or by writing:

Hampton Inn Fulfillment Center
P.O. Box 5266
Lincoln NE 68505-0266

Hilton   Hilton's HHonors Program for individuals age 60 and over comes with complementary membership for spouses, special services and HHonors bonus points for use toward exciting rewards. Some of the benefits include discounts from 25 to 50 percent off Hilton's current daily rate (location dependent) and it applies to either single or double occupancy.

The HHonors program also offers members the same discount on an extra room for your parents, children or grandchildren traveling with you. In addition, there is a 20 percent discount on dinner for two (whether you are a registered guest or not) at participating restaurants in more than 240 Hilton restaurants in the U.S. These benefits are also available at participating Hiltons in 32 countries.

They add nice touches like complimentary daily newspapers, late check-out and free use of health and recreational facilities (where available).

Hilton guarantees that your rates through the H-Honors program will be the lowest rates published for that hotel and they are lower than the hotel's AARP member rates. For example, in early 1990, the published daily rate at the Palmer House in Chicago was $165. However, Senior HHonors members paid only $60, a savings of $105.

If with 30 days you decide against using the program, you will receive a full refund of your membership fees. Annual fees are $25 for domestic membership and $50 for worldwide membership or $150 for lifetime worldwide membership.

Membership applications are available through travel advisors or by calling Hilton Reservations at 1-800-445-8667, ext. 901.

Holiday Inn   If you are a Mature Outlook member (see Chapter 11), you can save 20 percent off the cost of your room at participating Holiday Inns. Your children or grandchildren under age 12 (through teens in some hotels) will stay free with you in your room.

Whether you are staying there or not, your membership in Mature Outlook entitles you to a 10 percent discount for you and your guest at Holiday Inn Restaurants (excluding alcoholic beverages, gratuities, room service or tax). For more information, contact Mature Outlook (see Chapter 11).

Canadian Association of Retired Persons members will also find some discounts. Check with the Holiday Inn Burlington in Ontario for details.

Howard Johnson   If you have time to plan ahead, you can save 30 percent off the regular rate at Howard Johnson Hotels, Suites and Lodges. There are some limits on the number and type of rooms and some restrictions on the dates available, so you should call for your reservations as early as possible.

If your travel plans come up suddenly, you can still receive 15 percent off at participating Howard Johnson's, with no reservations required.

You can qualify for these discounts one of two ways. One is to be at least age 60. The other way is to be a member of a national senior's organization in the U.S. or the Canadian Association of Retired Persons.. If you are 50-59, check to see if they recognize the group you belong to when you call to make reservations at 1-800-634-3464.

La Quinta   They offer a 20% discount to guests age 60 or over who show their membership card in La Quinta's Senior Class at check-in. It only applies to rooms actually occupied by the person receiving the discount, but includes lodging for the third and fourth persons in your room if you want to travel with friends or family.

Check with the reservation clerks 1-800-531-5900 in the U.S. and Canada or 95-800-531-5900 in Mexico to verify the availability and amount of discounts available to you. There is a $10 annual fee for membership and applications are available at the hotels or by calling the reservation number above.

Marriott's   You can save 50 percent on your room rate at participating Marriott's if you are 62+ and belong to their Leisurelife Program. You need to make reservations in advance since the number of rooms available at these rates is limited. These discounts are usually available during off-peak periods, weekends, and holidays.

Joining the Leisurelife program is even more attractive because members can claim discounts of 25 percent on menu items at Marriott's restaurants (except advertised or menu-featured specials — other exclusions may apply). You can even use this meal discount at Marriott's when you are not staying at the hotel.

In addition, Leisurelife members are eligible for a 10 percent discount on applicable items at the gift shop purchases at participating Marriott's.

For reservations or more information, call Marriott's at 1- 800-228-9290 from the U.S. or Canada and ask for the Leisurelife Program rate.

Omni   At participating Omni Hotels, AARP members

can receive a 50 percent discount on the room rates and a 15 percent discount off food and non-alcoholic beverages. You will need to give your AARP membership number when you make your reservation and present your membership card when you check in. AARP members can call 1-800-THE-OMNI to check for discount availability and participating hotels.

Quality Inns   Participating Inns offer a 10 percent discount to National Association for Retired Credit Union People (NARCUP) members. If you are a member of the Canadian Association of Retired Persons (CARP), you are eligible for a 30 percent discount when you make a guaranteed reservation in the U.S. or Canada.

Ramada Inns   Participating Inns offer a 25 percent discount to National Association for Retired Credit Union People (NARCUP) members. They also recognize Canadian Association of Retired Persons (CARP) members and give them a discount. Call 1-800-228-2828.

Sheraton   You are offered a 25 percent discount off available room rates, requested and confirmed, except for rooms in the minimum rate category if you are age 60 and older and/or members of participating organizations including; American Association of Retired Persons (AARP), National Association of Retired Persons (NARP), Canadian Association of Retired Persons (CARP), National Retired Teachers Association (NRTA) and Retired Airline Employees Association (RAEA).

These discounts target travelers on pleasure-related, non-group travels. They cannot be used on rooms billed at a group discount or rooms already discounted under another program. As a special family benefit, you can have children age 17 or under stay free in your room as long as there is no need for additional bedding.

To make reservations, call 1-800-325-3535 and request the hotel, dates desired and the Retired Persons Discount. You will need to provide appropriate identification when you register at the hotel.

Westin   Probably the best discount program available is the one you can get at Westin Hotels and Resorts in Texas. If you are 60+, you can receive 50 percent off the room rate and an additional 10 percent discount on food and beverage. For information and reservations, call 1-800-228-3000.

AUTO RENTALS

There is a staggering variety of discount programs available on automobile rental. When you are making plans for your trip, you should consult with your travel agent. You may receive a better deal by booking a travel package that includes car rental as one part of that package. There may also be special promotions based on destination or time of the year.

Following are some of the major car rental firms along with the names of some of the organizations who say they have arrangements to get members a discount there. The phone numbers are for U.S. based calls. Since the reservations are often handled on a regional basis in Canada, check your phone book for the appropriate phone number from where you are.

Alamo Call 1-800-327-9633
>> National Association for Retired Credit Union People
>> September Days Club (Days Inns, etc.)

Avis Call 1-800-331-1212
>> American Association of Retired Persons
>> Mature Outlook (Sears)
>> National Alliance of Senior Citizens
>> National Association for Retired Credit Union People
>> National Senior Sports Association
>> Y.E.S. (Montgomery Ward)

Avis Canada
>> Canadian Association of Retired Persons

Budget Rent a Car Canada
>> Canadian Association of Retired Persons

Budget/Sears Call 1-800-527-0700
>> American Association of Retired Persons
>> Mature Outlook (both only at participating locations)

Hertz Call 1-800-654-3131
>> American Association of Retired Persons
>> Mature Outlook (Sears)
>> National Alliance of Senior Citizens

National Association for Retired Credit
Union People
National Senior Sports Association
Y.E.S. (Montgomery Ward)

Hertz Penske Rental Trucks
Y.E.S. (Montgomery Ward)

National Call 1-800-328-4567
Mature Outlook
National Alliance of Senior Citizens
National Association for Retired Credit
Union People
National Senior Sports Association
Y.E.S. (Montgomery Ward)

AIRLINES

The airlines know that as a mature traveler, you want more than just the ability to get from one point to another. You appreciate value, service, and comfort in your travels.

Many airlines have designed special programs to attract your business by making your travel more convenient and luxurious. By using these programs, you are eligible for wonderful benefits that other travelers only dream of.

A lot of airlines give a standard 10 percent discount for those they consider seniors. Fortunately, while that is great, it is only the beginning.

If you need more information on any of the programs mentioned below, or want to see if another airline you use regularly has a similar plan, you can ask your travel agent or call the reservations number for that airline as listed in the yellow pages of your phone book.

Change Your Plans
Without Forfeiting Your Money

If you have ever set up a trip and then had to cancel at the last minute, you have experienced that sinking feeling when you realize you may have forfeited your airfare. At British Airways, members of their Privileged Traveller Program traveling on British Airways will have any monetary fee associated with the pre-trip change or cancellation of the reservation waived. Members can also receive 10 percent discounts on round-trip or one-way British Airways airfares purchased in the U.S.

The Privileged Traveller Card is available to U.S. customers who are 60 or older. There is a $10 handling fee for processing and no renewal fees will be charged to card holders who have flown on British Airways during the life of the Card. For an application or more information, call 1-800-AIRWAYS.

Have you ever belonged to one of those airline frequent-flier clubs? Whenever you traveled on that airline, your mileage credits would build up until you could cash them in on a free ticket or other benefit. At Northwest Airlines, you will find their WorldPerks Senior Club offers you mileage benefits and a whole lot more to travelers age 62 or older. This great deal includes: savings on vacation packages; hotel, car rental and cruise discounts; periodic discounts to select destinations; and exciting tour packages designed especially for you.

Oh yes. The mileage. For every 20,000 miles, you will automatically receive two 10,000 mile Fly-Write tickets which you can use for free round trip travel or as First Class upgrades within the 48 contiguous United States or Canada. As your mileage benefits add up, you can qualify for free travel to Alaska, Hawaii, the Caribbean, Mexico, Europe and Asia.

To make sure you find out about all their current and upcoming programs, your WorldPerks membership includes a quarterly newsletter with all the latest news.

One other benefit that may be attractive, especially if you hate waiting in those crowded, noisy seating areas in the airport, is the discount on the membership fee in their WorldClubs. These private club rooms in the airports offer gracious hospitality and on-duty staffing to help make your travel more comfortable.

COUPON BOOKS CAN BE A GREAT DEAL

One benefit that has been around for a while (and probably under-utilized) is the coupon book. However, part of the problem may have been the concept of paying a fee for travel you may — or may not — take in the future.

At Delta Airlines, you have the opportunity to purchase their Young-At-Heart Fares if you are at least 62 years old. In early 1990, you could purchase a book of eight coupons for just $704. These coupons allow you to travel with a reserved seat any day, to any Delta or Delta Connection city in the continental U. S. and Puerto Rico for only one coupon ($88 each way).

There are some other restrictions and the offer does

not include certain fees or taxes. However, all you have to do is make your reservations at least 14 days before your departure. Once your coupon is validated, there is a cash penalty for voluntary change or cancellation of your travel plans.

The coupons in your book are good for one year from your date of purchase — but they are only valid for the person named on the book. This kind of coupon offer is also offered by other airlines including American. Terms and conditions may differ from one airline to another.

Delta offers another benefit that is especially attractive to those hate to travel alone. Along with the 10 percent discount for passengers 62 or older, traveling partners for those ticketed passengers can also receive a 10 percent discount on their ticket — regardless of their age. Is there someplace special you always wanted to share with your child or grandchild?

What are you waiting for?

AFFINITY GROUPS AID TRAVEL PLANS

Sometimes the best deal on an airline may be one offered through an organization you belong to. At American Airlines (1-800-433-7300), members of AARP (starting at age 50, much younger than most other mature traveler discounts) enjoy benefits not available to others. AARP members are eligible to fly at a 10 percent discount off the lowest round-trip individual discount air fare.

There are some restrictions including that you make your reservations at least 30 days in advance and stay at your destination over a Saturday night. If you change your plans after making your reservation, you are subject to a maximum 50 percent penalty. Other restrictions may apply.

Sometimes the details of your discount may vary with age and destination. At Canadian Airlines International (1-800-426-7000 from the U.S), some discounts are available at age 55, but you can not qualify for others until you are 62. The details are complicated, so you will need to talk to a reservations clerk to determine what discounts might be available for your itinerary. If you are calling their reservations people from Canada, you will need to check the local phone book for the correct phone number in your area.

As you are making your travel plans, remember that specific discount offers can come and go in the blink of an eye. Even the programs offered by major firms are subject to change. As this book is going to press, United Airlines SilverWings Plus (1-800-628-2868) program is undergoing a major renovation. Details of the new programs should be available by the fall of 1990 by calling that phone number.

These travel discount programs can be wonderful deals which enable you to travel more often, more comfortably and to places you never thought you would have a chance to experience. If an airline you want to fly does not have a program listed here, do not be shy. Ask. They may very well have something that will interest you. If not, at least you have given them something to think about.

REBATES

Some organizations which offer travel services also will give you a rebate of part of your travel costs. To receive the rebate, you must book your travel through their travel service and it must be travel for which the travel service earns a commission from the service provider.

The amounts of the rebate will typically be about three percent of the pretax cost of the applicable travel items. You will receive a rebate form from the travel service, and you can apply for it after your travel is complete.

There are some organizations which offer rebates through their programs. They include the National Association for Retired Credit Union People and the Y.E.S. program offered through Montgomery Ward. You can contact them at the addresses and/or phone numbers given for them in Chapter 11.

OTHER RESOURCES

Now that you have an idea about what kinds of programs you can find to save you money on travel and accommodations, you are ready to look further.

One way is to contact the companies mentioned here, get their literature and compare programs to your personal travel style and goals. If you have a travel agent you frequently work with, he or she might be able to point out programs which would suit your individual needs.

There is also another book out which primarily deals with getting good deals and discounts on your travel. *Unbelievably Good Deals & Great Adventures That You*

Absolutely Can't Get Unless You're Over 50 by Joan Rattner Heilman is a treasure trove of not only discounts, but wonderful adventures that are available to you. It is available in many bookstores and libraries.

CHAPTER 9: DISCOUNTS ON RECREATIONAL ACTIVITIES

"We do not stop playing because we are old.
We grow old because we stop playing."
- Author unknown

Making the most of life includes taking time for yourself. In years past, your concerns about family and career matters probably kept you from having much time for recreation.

Now you have more control over your schedule. If you could choose (and your can!) will you continue to enjoy pastimes which have brought you a lot of pleasure in the past? Or would you choose adventures or sports you always dreamed about and can indulge yourself in now?

Here in North America, you have a smorgasbord of recreational activities available to you. What makes them even more attractive is that many recreationally oriented businesses will gladly give you a discount on the price if you just ask.

Once again, a major reason they are interested in you is because you are part of an active and growing age group. You have more time to enjoy sports — and you are willing to buy the equipment you need to play your best. For instance, the Sporting Goods Manufacturer

Association estimates that people age 55 and older spent $174,800,000 on golf equipment alone in 1986. That same year, you and your peers spent nearly $110,000,000 on exercise equipment.

All of the money you have been willing to invest in sporting equipment means you are seen as BIG business in the sporting arena.

ACTIVE SPORTS — GO FOR THE GUSTO

Remember, whatever the sport, they do not call them "Masters' " tournaments for nothing. As you mature, you can see that your accumulated experience can help you be better at your favorite sports than you were in your 30s and 40s.

If your sport is golf, tennis or bowling, the National Senior Sports Association (NSSA) could help you save money on everything from game fees to equipment. It offers you discounts and group travel programs to play your sport in places you may have only dreamed of.

For instance, if you are a golfer, you can go on its "Sports Holidays Abroad" program and play the famous courses of Scotland, Ireland, and other spectacular courses.

NSSA organizes and conducts recreational and competitive tournaments where players are grouped by skill levels. By utilizing its group purchasing power and off-season scheduling NSSA can offer extremely attractive package plans.

Even non-playing spouses enjoy the trip because of the full range of planned activities for them at every event.

NSSA membership can save you money on your

sports hobbies even when you are not traveling, If your game is golf, you can get a special discount on Hale Irwin's Golfers' Passport which provides discounts at more than 1,400 golf courses and resorts. The Passport entitles you to play the courses twice a year with no green fees. You pay the cart rental only.

Bowlers will find that their NSSA membership entitles them to a 10 percent discount on bowling balls, bags, shoes and other merchandise at any Brunswick Bowling Center.

If NSSA sounds like your idea of fun, the membership information is in Chapter 11.

ON YOUR OWN

What if you enjoy playing your sport locally and prefer not to join a group? Many sports facilities offer you a discount when you play. Just be sure to ask before you pay or play.

Skiers tend to be a friendly but independent lot, and the discounts that are available to you as a skier are very individualized by the resort you choose.

The age you become eligible ranges from about 55 up to 70 depending on the resort. The discounts can be as little as a few dollars off the regular weekend rates. But then, some discounts can be substantial, like offering a season pass for only the processing costs. Some, like Squaw Valley in the Lake Tahoe Basin, charge only a nominal fee. In the 1989-90 season, skiers age 13 to 64 paid $38 for a full day of skiing. Yet, skiers who were 65 or older only paid $5.

Of course, the best discounts are the resorts which allow you to ski for free. At Mammoth in Southern

California, you can ski for free once you are 65 or older. That compares with an adult one-day rate of $35 in the 1989-90 season.

At least one facility has developed an innovative deal to attract you — and build future business at the same time. At Lake Reba, in 1989-90 they offered a free pass for a grandchild age 12 or younger with each grandparent who skied Sunday through Friday. This program was very successful, and will be offered again.

Because each resort has its own program, and because there are so many places to ski throughout the country, you should work with your travel agent to find the resort which offers you the best discount.

When you make your plans, check to see what the correct procedure for getting your discount. At some places, you may have to go to a special window to receive your free or discount passes.

AROUND AND ABOUT

Every time you travel, you have an opportunity to visit the sights and events that make your destination so special. But sometimes you can have a problem finding out what kinds of tourism activities are available.

If you belong to a motor club, check to see if they offer tour books or other information to help you plan what you want to see.

There is one wonderful, free deal that can help you — and you do not even have to be 50. The Travel Industry Association of America will send you a list of state and territorial tourism offices, complete with addresses and phone numbers.

When you have this information and decide to travel to Kentucky on business or to Illinois to visit family, you can contact the state tourism office to get information about any sights, festivals or activities that work with your schedule and whim.

To get this list, write or call:

Travel Industry Association of America
Two Lafayette Centre
1133 21st Street, NW
Washington, DC 20036 (202) 293-1433

As you plan your recreational travel, keep in mind that many communities make a special effort to attract you and show you a good time.

Some of the special programs may be offered in what could be called the off-season, but that does not mean it is a bad time to travel there. Many vacation destinations go off-season when school starts and families find it more difficult to travel.

However, if you have the freedom to travel then, you may find that smaller crowds, more moderate temperatures and off-season rates make it the best time of all to be there.

HISTORIC WILLIAMSBURG

At Williamsburg, Virginia there is a community-wide program called Senior Time in September. As a salute to those 55 or older, Senior Time includes special offers and rates at hotels, motels, bed & breakfast lodgings, attractions, restaurants, camp-grounds, shops and other businesses. The Williamsburg area is an incredible historical resource. While you are there you can enjoy everything from a re-creation of the Jamestown

Settlement and Colonial Williamsburg to a Fife and Drum Parade and the Williamsburg Winery.

For more information and a brochure, write to:

Williamsburg Area Convention
and Visitors Bureau
P.O. Box GB
Williamsburg, Virginia 23187

SAVE MONEY EVEN IN
THE GREAT OUTDOORS

Our federal, state and local parklands are a direct legacy of people like President Theodore Roosevelt and John Muir, whose dedication to open spaces built the foundation for the benefits we enjoy today.

On the federal level, there are some parks, refuges and facilities which can be entered and used free of charge. Others require payment of entrance fees, user fees, special recreation permit fees or some combination thereof.

If you are under age 62, you can get a great deal on recreation by purchasing the Golden Eagle Pass which is an annual entrance pass to those national parks, monuments, historic sites, recreation areas and national wildlife refuges that charge entrance fees.

This $25 pass will get you and any accompanying passengers in your private, non-commercial vehicle onto the site. Where entry is not by private vehicle, the pass will still get you, your spouse, children and parents into the site. The Golden Eagle Pass does not cover user fees which are charged in some areas for the use of certain facilities such as campgrounds, specialized boat launching equipment, cave tours, etc.

Once you have it, you can use this pass as many times as you wish during the year. Since single-visit entrance fees range from $1 to $4 per person or $3 to $10 per carload at these attractions, you can see how quickly you can recoup your $25 investment and begin saving money.

You can buy a Golden Eagle Pass in person at all National Park Service and U.S. Forest Service headquarters and regional offices.

Once you hit 62, then you can *really* get a great deal. You are now eligible for the Golden Age Passport which entitles you to free lifetime entrance to all the places mentioned above that charge entrance fees.

There is more! Your Golden Age Passport entitles you to a 50 percent discount on federal use fees charged for facilities and services — although it does not cover fees charged by private concessionaires. This Passport admits the same people with you as the Golden Eagle Pass with one exception. It does not include your parents. But then, they are eligible for their own Golden Age Passport anyway!

You need to apply for your Golden Age Passport in person at most federally operated recreation areas where it may be used. Be sure to have proof of your age like a driver's license with you.

If you want more information, you can contact a local federally operated recreational facility (under U.S. Government in your phone book) or write to:

U.S. Department of the Interior
National Park Service
P.O. Box 37127
Washington, DC 20013

STATE YOUR PREFERENCE

Not only federal facilities offer you a cash discount. You should also check with your state (and any state you are interested in visiting) to see what kind of special programs they offer you. For instance, in New York State, residents who are 62 or older can get great deals on any weekdays (except holidays) can access these money-saving benefits:

- Free vehicle access to state parks and arboretums

- Free entrance to state historic sites

- 50% fee reduction for state-operated swimming, golf, tennis and boat rental.

This is one of those programs that not only offers cash benefits — they have pity on how thick your wallet has become. You do not need a special identification card. Your valid New York State Driver's License or Non-Driver's Identification Card will give you access to these benefits.

Further information on this New York State program can be had by writing to:

State Parks
Albany, NY 12238

UNDER THE STARS

Hotels and motels are marvelous places. But if you love the great outdoors, there is nothing like camping to get the most out of your travels.

At Safari Campgrounds and Yogi Bear Jellystone Camp Resorts, each facility is independently owned as a franchise, and the majority of them offer discounts to mature travelers. They can accommodate recreational vehicles, pop-ups, tents, and some parks have RV and cabin rentals available for campers who like to travel light.

To find out about parks where you plan to travel and to ask about discount programs, call them at 1-800-558-2954.

HALF THE FUN IS GETTING THERE

As you well know, sometimes the way you make the journey is what makes it so much fun.

Traveling in a motor home is one way you can stop and smell the flowers, enjoy the sunsets and experience every attraction along your travel route.

You can save when traveling by motorhomes when you rent your vehicle through the over 200 locations of Cruise America (1-800-327-7778). If you are an AARP member, you are eligible for 10 percent off the time and mileage charges as well as 10 percent off the mandatory vehicle preparation fees at all rental locations in the U.S. and Canada. You will even be covered by more third-party liability insurance than the minimum that applies to non-AARP members.

Another way to travel that certainly is a kind of recreation all by itself is by train. Amtrak offers some wonderful fares to help you see America. Once you are age 65, you are entitled to 25 percent off the price of its regular fares. If you are younger and disabled, you are also eligible for this fare. (You will need some documentation of your disability.)

When you talk with your travel agent or the reservation clerk for Amtrak, ask about other discounts that may not be age-related. Sometimes you can save even more with them. For more information or reservations, you can call Amtrak at: 1-800-USA-RAIL.

A HELPING HAND

Whether you are traveling in a rented motor home or in one you own, the lure of the open road can be hard to resist. One organization which makes it even easier to give in to this temptation is the Good Sam Club.

Although there is no minimum age requirement to join the Good Sam Club (1-800-234-3450; see Chapter 11 for more information), people who have the time to travel extensively by recreational vehicle tend to be those who are done raising their families.

As a Good Sam Club member, you have access to a number of valuable — and in some cases unique — services. Some of the services are things you might expect like the trip routing service, full-service travel agency, travelers checks, magazine, etc.

The additional services help ease some of the fears you may have had about traveling in a motor home. One of the most comforting services is the Lost Pet Service. If your pet runs off while you are on the road, the special Good Sam tag you have put on its collar will tell its rescuer to call Good Sam so they can help reunite you with your pet.

If you are planning an extended trip, you will be concerned about receiving your mail. Good Sam's Mail Forwarding Service can collect and forward your mail to whereever you expect to be — and you only pay the postage.

Take advantage of these wonderful deals and discounts — and look for others where ever you go to have fun. You deserve to enjoy yourself.

CHAPTER 10:
HOW TO CONVINCE LOCAL MERCHANTS TO OFFER DISCOUNTS

"What we have here is a failure to communicate."
*Donn Pearce, **Cool Hand Luke**, screenplay, 1967*

When a local business you patronize does not offer you a discount, then the problem may very well be a failure to communicate. If so, there are some specific steps you can take to enhance this communication and increase your chances of saving money when you do business there.

Remember, you are not coming hat in hand to ask for a handout. You are giving the business owner a chance to increase his or her income by attracting new customers — including you.

You and your peers constitute a fast growing segment of the population. According to studies reported by S. Amanda Putnam, Carl E. Steidtmann and the Management Horizons Division of Price Waterhouse in their 55 Plus, you are more likely than the general population to enjoy discretionary income, especially if you are between the ages of 55 and 64.

Also remember that even if a particular business does not seem to be oriented toward your needs, you and your peers may do more shopping there than you think. You might not automatically think of toy stores when you think of mature discounts, but the 55 Plus study discovered that grandparents are estimated to be the source of almost 25 percent of the dollars spent on children's toys — or about $250 per year on gifts for grandchildren.

A GREAT EXAMPLE

If, at sometime, you are tempted to give up and not ask for your discount, remember Roy Fannin.

Roy lives in Columbus, Ohio, and is a retired pastry baker. He admits to saving thousands of dollars by using discounts over the last few years. The primary way he saves so much is by using his Golden Buckeye Card which entitles him to discounts at thousands of businesses in Ohio.

He says, "A penny saved is a penny earned — especially on a fixed income." So he is careful to patronize auto shops, restaurants, hardware stores and other businesses which offer him a discount. He says that most businesses will give a discount if you just ask — even if they do not have a discount program posted in their business.

If you are interested in a discount, Roy adds that sometimes you can even convince a merchant to expand his posted policies if it would meet your needs. He remembers a time when he wanted to purchase some patio furniture. The furniture sale — and a friend who would haul the furniture home for him — both came together a day before the store's weekly discount day. The clerk initially told him he could not have the discount, but just then the manager walked by.

You guessed it. Within minutes the manager authorized the 10 percent discount on the $400 of patio furniture and Roy was on his way — with his $40 savings in his pocket. Can you do the same thing? Probably.

The only way you will find out is to ask.

GETTING STARTED

Obviously, when you have decided that you would like to receive a discount at a particular business is to ask if they already have one. You may be pleasantly surprised to find they are way ahead of you. For whatever reason, many businesses which offer discounts do not post signs telling you about them, but they will be very helpful once you ask.

If you find that there is no discount at that time, you can swing into action. First, realize that the clerk you are dealing with probably has no way of changing things. So if you are told there is no program, do not waste your time and the clerk's by explaining the benefits of offering discounts.

You *should* ask the clerk for the name of the manager/owner of the business. Then contact that person either in person or by letter to let him know that you believe the business should offer a discount.

Resist the temptation to "come on too strong." This is an informational contact. If you listen carefully, the owner/manager may tell you the business's reasons for not offering discounts. And that will tell you what you need to know so you can change the policy.

If the reason is that their profit margin is too tight and they would lose money if they gave discounts, you may not be able to be successful. However, if you are that business owner or you want to help him build his business, there are still things that can be done to increase its attractiveness to mature shoppers. For instance, some stores are already offering services other than discounts, like electric carts patrons can use while they are shopping. Others are distributing informational pamphlets to help their customers.

What if the business owner does not offer a discount because he or she does not believe there is a demand? There is a lot you can do to convince your contact that the demand is there. Talk to your friends and members of organizations you belong to. You could start a letter writing campaign or get petitions signed. If you belong to a local senior center, retirement club or other age-specific organization, there may already be a staff person or officer who contacts businesses and explains the benefits of offering discounts. Perhaps your organization can offer the businessperson the opportunity for free advertising when your group mentions the business's new discounts in your newsletter.

GO FOR IT!

Does it really make a difference if you ask for a discount? The answer is a resounding yes. In the research for this book, there were restaurants, service businesses and others who were flirting with the idea of having a discounting program to attract mature customers.

One thing they are looking for is feedback that this is something you want. You may never know how important your letter or phone call was in helping the marketing people at a company decide that you deserved a better deal.

Everyone tends to think of discounting decisions coming from some distant corporate office, but the truth is that a surprising number of businesses are either franchises or completely independent businesses that are owned by someone in your community. These people are anxious to serve their neighbors and will be especially interested in your efforts to convince them to offer discounts.

However, if you are reluctant to approach your local merchant — or if you do not receive the welcome you deserve — you should write to the customer relations manager at the corporate office. (If you do not know where it is, your librarian can get that information for you.) These people are very interested in how you feel about their company. In most companies, they will try to work with you to help smooth the relationship between their business and your community.

AND THE ANSWER IS . . .

There are some questions you are likely to face when you approach a business to get to convince them to offer you and your peers a discount. Be sure you have thought through the answers you want to give before you contact them. Remember to add facts you know about your local marketplace and personalize your answers so they reflect the businessowner's needs.

- *Why should I offer discounts?*

Depending on your community, you could take one of two positions. If you are in an affluent area, use the figures from Chapter 1 of this book to show how strong your buying power is. Your local agency on aging may be able to give you accurate figures about the number and affluence of mature consumers in your area.

If you live in an area where people have not had so many opportunities to accumulate assets, you can reason with the business owner as another person who has worked hard and now needs to make the most of what they have worked for. It can also be seen as a way of thanking those whose hard work has built your community over the years.

- *How much will it cost me?*

Savvy business owners realize that giving a discount is not the same as giving away money. Properly designed, a discount will bring in new customers, increase sales, and increase loyalty from long-time customers.

- *When should I offer the discount?*

If the business owner you are trying to convince has to deal with uneven periods of customer demand, you may be able to help. Suggest that the discount or deal be offered only during his slack days of the week or hours of the day.

For example, Sizzler Restaurants offer afternoon discounts to those 55 or over. This way the restaurant brings in customers who want the discount and enjoy the more relaxed pace during those hours.

And remember the Ace Hardware store mentioned in Chapter 3? The owner was able to revitalize his slow Wednesdays by making that the discount day — and his business has profited from it.

- *How can I keep my younger customers from*

getting upset?

Certainly, one way is to offer a discount for all ages — like the "Early Bird" dinners at some restaurants. However, many businesses handle this problem through their advertising. When they advertise in the mainstream press or radio, they do not mention the mature customer discounts. However, when they advertise in magazines, newspapers, direct mail and other outlets which are targeted strictly to mature readers, they prominently mention their discounting program.

- *Why should I target mature shoppers?*

Some businesses never stop to realize how many mature customers they have. They have gotten so accustomed to hearing that the Baby Boomers are where their best market is, that they may be missing the market that is right under their nose. In 1988, the 55 Plus market represented over $900 billion in consumer spending according to Price Waterhouse's "55 Plus" study.

The study found that households headed by 55 to 64 year olds exceeded average spending in the categories of: food, both at home and away from home; alcohol; tobacco, women's and girls' apparel; gas and motor oil; public transportation; health and personal care; and fees and admissions. Spending by households headed by those 65 or older also exceeded the average in many of these categories.

Why should the business offer you a discount? Because it simply makes good sense. By letting you and your peers know that he values your patronage enough to offer you a discount, the business owner will be bringing new lifeblood into his business.

WORKING TOGETHER GIVES YOU BARGAINING POWER

By yourself, you may be able to convince a business owner to offer a discounting program based on your convincing arguments. However, according to Ridge Eagan, Advertising Director for *Senior Spectrum* (published in 19 editions in three states), your chances of convincing a business owner to offer a discount will be much better if you are asking as the representative of a group. He says that the owner is more likely to be convinced if you can show him a ready-made base of potential customers.

The group you are representing could be your local senior center, retirement club, or other age-specific organization. If they do not currently have a committee to help get discounts, perhaps you can start one.

After all, your group can offer the business owner a lot of potential customers, word-of-mouth referrals to others, and free advertising, especially if your group keeps a list of locally offered discounts or mentions them in their newsletter.

Do not get discouraged if your first effort to convince a business owner to offer a discount is less than successful. If you persist, you will ultimately succeed. Maybe not with the first business — but with one which had not been offering a discount before. Just think how it will feel when you have been the one who has made it possible for many people to save money on their purchases, thus improving their lifestyle.

Go for the gusto. You can make a positive difference in your world today!

CHAPTER 11: GROUPS AND PUBLICATIONS

"Union gives strength."
Aesop, **The Bundle of Sticks**

The urge to join together with others who share your needs and goals is probably as old as mankind. That certainly does not change just because you mature.

In fact, because you are mature, you are undoubtedly more discriminating in your choice of groups you are interested in. Here are some organizations which are designed especially for mature people. Some will be more familiar than others.

You will find that occasionally the goods or services mentioned as being benefits of these organizations may be available to you separately. Check the appropriate chapter (as in Chapter 6 for mail order pharmacies) to see which providers may be able to serve you independently.

Because of space limitations and the fact that these organizations are always striving to find new ways to serve their members, these listings do not include every benefit offered by every group. This is only an overview to give you a feeling about which groups interests and benefits might help you.

If any of these sound tempting to you, please write or call them at the addresses and telephone numbers listed and they will send you more information.

Hint: to save some money and time (if there are several of these organizations you want to contact), consider using the pre-stamped postcards available at the post office to quickly jot off a request for more information to each organization.

Here are the organizations in alphabetical order.

AMERICAN ASSOCIATION OF
RETIRED PERSONS

The American Association of Retired Persons (AARP) has over 31 million members, making it the largest organization of its kind. It was founded in 1958 by the late Dr. Ethel Percy Andrus, a retired educator. Her goals for the organization included: enhance the qualify of life for older persons; promote the independence, dignity and purpose for older persons; lead in determining the role and place of older persons in society; and improve the image of aging.

Over the years, AARP has developed a smorgasbord of opportunities for its members. They include health, car, and homeowner insurance programs, a credit union, an investment program, a motor club, a pharmacy service and a variety of travel related services. These programs are detailed in their respective chapters in this book.

There are many special advocacy programs which invite participation by AARP members. You might choose to become involved with a group working to inform older voters on key issues and candidates' announced positions. Maybe you would like to volunteer to work with boards and commissions in your area to increase the presence of older citizens. Or perhaps you would feel more useful working with others to help make Congress and the Administration aware of the nation's needs for a comprehensive policy on long-term care.

If you are not sure what you would like to do, then one thing you could do as an AARP member would be to register with the AARP Volunteer Talent Bank which will match your skills with the needs of programs through AARP and other organizations. There are more than 3,700 AARP chapters and 2,500 Retired Teacher Association units throughout the country, and you may find activities of interest through your chapter contacts.

Part of saving money, and that is the focus of this book, is recognizing resources and making use of them. In addition to its community service program, AARP offers members:

- Consumer Affairs Program - Helps older people become more knowledgeable consumers of goods and services. Publishes information on finances, utilities, housing, funerals, and other consumer topics.

- Criminal Justice Services - Offers programs to help older persons reduce or remove opportunities for victimization and trains older persons to work with law enforcement officials.

- 55 Alive/Mature Driving - The nation's first driver retraining program specifically designed for motorists age 55 and older. This eight-hour classroom course uses volunteer instructors and audio-visual materials.

- Health Advocacy Services - Provides information

about health promotion, disease prevention and long-term care. Program volunteers also help older consumers use the Medicare system and the health care marketplace to their best advantage.

- Housing Program - Offers information on housing options to consumers and providers. Serves as liaison with other private organizations and government agencies concerned with housing for the elderly.

- Institute of Lifetime Learning - Enhances opportunities for continuing education for older persons by working with the academic community, developing curriculums, and providing a wide range of informational and educational materials.

- Intergenerational Program - Designed to help children and youth better appreciate the concerns, skills and lifestyles of older persons. Resources include publications for teachers, agencies, librarians, and program plan developer, as well as a "Growing Up - Growing Older," film series.

- International Activities - Produces, distributes and promotes the exchange of information about older people worldwide through the International Federation on Aging which AARP helped found in 1973. Today, IFA has 88 member organizations representing older persons from 45 countries; AARP sponsors IFA's Publications Division.

- Interreligious Liaison - Assists religious organizations and ecumenical and interfaith agencies in developing programs involving older persons in both congregational and community activities.

- Legal Counsel for the Elderly - Provides free legal services to older residents of the District of Columbia; operates a national training program for attorneys and other advocates; recruits volunteers for advocacy programs nationwide; is testing a legal "Hotline" in Pittsburgh, PA; operates a home study paralegal course; publishes legal materials for attorneys as well as older people themselves; and operates volunteer programs to assist older people with their financial affairs in various communities nationally.

- National Gerontology Resource Center - Furnishes information on aging and the older population to interested organizations, institutions, government agencies and the news media. Located at AARP national headquarters, the Center includes an extensive library collection on social gerontology and retirement.

- NRTA Activities - National Retired Teachers Association Division serves as national liaison to state retired teachers associations and other education-oriented groups in making available the resources of AARP through its NRTA Division.

- Senior Community Service Employment Program - Trains economically disadvantaged older persons and helps place them in permanent jobs. Funded by the U.S. Labor Department, the new program now has offices in more than 110 sites in 33 states and Puerto Rico. Also works with the Environmental Protection Agency on programs dealing with noise pollution and asbestos monitoring.

- Tax Aide Program - Helps more than a million older Americans prepare their tax forms each year. This free public service uses volunteer tax counselors trained by AARP in cooperation with the Internal Revenue Service.

- Widowed Persons Service - Provides organizational and training resources to local groups interested in community-wide programs to serve newly widowed persons. Local services may include volunteer outreach, telephone referral, group meetings, public education, and a resource directory.

AARP has a library of over 140 publications which they offer free or for a nominal fee to members. The topics include:

> Caregiving
> Crime Prevention
> Government
> Health/Lifestyle
> Housing
> Learning
> Legal Rights (nominal fee)
> Life Planning
> Money
> Retirement Planning
> Volunteers
> Women
> Work

The best known publication of AARP is their bimonthly magazine, *Modern Maturity*. AARP also publishes the *AARP Bulletin* in a newspaper format to keep members up-to-date on the latest news on current events, important legislation, member activities, etc.

Access to all the benefits above is available to you for the annual membership fee of $5 (which includes your spouse) and $7 per year for people living outside the U.S. Mail limits. Membership is open to anyone who is at least 50 years of age. While the name says it is an organization of retired persons, you do not have to wait to retire to join. AARP figures show that one-third of the Association's members are older workers.

If you are interested in joining AARP, send your name, address, date of birth and a check for $5 ($7 if you live outside U.S. Mail limits) to:

American Association of Retired Persons
Membership Processing Center
P.O. Box 199
Long Beach, CA 90848-9900

ASSOCIATION OF RETIRED AMERICANS

The Association of Retired Americans (ARA) was founded just to help you get special deals and discounts. As a member, you become eligible for a variety of great discount programs.

Prescription drugs are available by mail through Advanced Prescription Service. With the purchase of three prescriptions or more, they also offer you your choice of one of four varieties of over-the-counter vitamins.

ARA's hearing aid service offers members premium quality hearing aids on a no-risk, satisfaction-guaranteed basis. Members with a prescription for a specific hearing aid can call their toll-free number to receive a price quote.

ARA participates in Opticare 2000, an optical care program designed specifically to handle the eye care needs of mature people. The benefits include free vision screenings for cataracts, glaucoma and visual acuity, discounts on eye glasses, Medicare assignments, 24 hour emergency services, referral services, 25 percent discounts on comprehensive eye exams and office visits and even free round trip transportation.

Another member benefit is a laminated personal medical identification card which is free to the primary member and available at a discount for family, friends and associates. In a medical emergency, this card will make information about your doctor's name, medical history, current medications and allergies readily available.

ARA offers two other distinct benefits for members who love to read. First is their *Vintage Times*, a bimonthly journal of news, commentary, features and consumer information designed to be of interest to you.

The other reader's benefit is membership in a large-print book club. The books have a typeface which is nearly double that of conventional type, making them easier to read. All kinds of books are available including best sellers, romance, mystery, fiction, reference, and even children's books. As an ARA member, you will receive a 25 percent discount on all of your purchases.

Membership in ARA is open to anyone age 50 or older. The $30 per year includes you and your spouse. For more information contact them at:

Association of Retired Americans
206 East College
Grapevine, Texas 76051
1-800-622-8040

CANADIAN ASSOCIATION OF
RETIRED PERSONS

The Canadian Association of Retired Persons (CARP) is an exciting membership organization open to everyone, not just Canadians. Like AARP, you can join at age 50, and you do not have to be retired.

CARP benefits range into all areas. The organization advocates on housing and other issues of concern to its members before the provincial and federal government bodies. They make group insurance available in a number of areas including homeowners, automobile, hospital, travel and a cancer plan which covers many other diseases too.

As a member, you can take advantage of discounts on health items like prescription eyewear (glasses, contact lenses, etc.) throughout the country. There is also a program to help members get discounts on hearing aids.

If you are interested in financial benefits, you want to know about CARP's discount brokerages investment services. In addition, members can apply for a very special VISA card. Once you have been approved for this card, you automatically receive one year's free membership in CARP (a $10 value which will be used to pay this year's fees if due, or extend your membership one year). Along with your card, you will receive vouchers worth $400 off TD Bank services. And if that is not enough to convince you, they even lowered the interest rate by 0.5 percent on outstanding balances for CARP members.

If you are thinking about traveling, your CARP membership entitles you to discounts at Budget Rent-a-Car of Canada, Avis Canada, and many hotels including Quality Inns, Clarion Hotels, Marriott Hotels, Sheratons, Relax Plaza Hotels and Inns and others. If you are planning travel in the U.S., CARP says that your membership card will be honored almost everywhere that the AARP card is accepted.

CARP has chapters throughout the country and new ones are forming all the time. They are also working to provide practical assistance to members. In 1990 they offered their first Job Fair which was so successful that the turnout overwhelmed the employers who were there. Plans are being made to expand this program and possibly have some local chapters put on a similar event.

To keep up with all their news and events, CARP members receive a quarterly newspaper in a tabloid format. Along with news about membership activities and benefits, there are articles targeting health, employment and other issues.

Membership costs $10 per year or $25 for three years. For more information, contact CARP at:

Canadian Association of Retired Persons
27 Queen Street East, Suite 304
Toronto, Ontario M5C 2M6

CLUB 55

Club 55 is a tremendous package of benefits for

members who bank through the Citizens Fidelity Bank & Trust Company of Kentucky and Indiana. The Club identification card is free, and it entitles you to goodies like:

- Free personalized checks
- Interest on your checking account — regardless of your balance
- A special high-rate savings account
- Free travelers checks
- Preferred rates on installment loans
- Discount pharmacy service
- Key ring protection
- Discounts on travel and recreation
- $100,000 Accidental Death Insurance (when traveling on a licensed common carrier)
- Bonus travel program
- Financial newsletter
- 24-hour banking
- Credit card protection

Obviously, there is a minimum age for this program, and it is 55. If you live in Kentucky this could be a great program and save you a lot of money. If you do not live in Kentucky, check with several financial institutions in your area to see if they have a program similar to this. If not, do not be shy, ask. Sometimes the businesses just need to know the demand is there.

For more detailed information on this program, write to:

Program Director - Club 55
Citizens Fidelity Bank & Trust Company
Citizens Plaza
Louisville, KY 40296
(502) 581-7048

GOLDEN BUCKEYE

If you live in Ohio or are thinking about moving there, this program can save you *lots* of money. Ohioans age 60 and over and/or those Ohioans age 18 or over who have been certified totally and permanently disabled can use their Golden Buckeye Card to purchase goods and services at discounted prices from participating businesses which have volunteered to give discounts to cardholders.

There are thousands of participating businesses. Each decides on the definition of the discount they will offer. while 10 percent is often the choice, some choose 5 percent or 20 percent. Some businesses restrict their discount to one or more days per week. Some restrict the discount to certain products like tire purchases or lighting fixtures. Others offer free services which are specific to their businesses like a chiropractor who offers a free spinal exam or attorneys who offer a free initial consultation.

The program began in 1976, and has been improved several times since then. There are sites throughout the state where residents can apply for their card — or get information about the program. For more specific information, contact them at:

The Ohio Department of Aging
Golden Buckeye Card Program
600 E. 11th Avenue
Columbus, Ohio 43211

GOLDEN MOUNTAINEER

West Virginia has another state-specific program which offers residents some wonderful deals and discounts. Residents who have a valid driver's license receive their Golden Mountaineer membership card automatically at their 60th birthday. Those who do not drive can get the card at their local senior center or at the West Virginia Commission on Aging.

Like the Golden Buckeye program, merchants and service providers decide what benefits they will provide. Program headquarters ask that participating businesses put up a poster describing what benefits they offer and display a decal.

This program was begun in 1980 by then-governor John D. Rockefeller IV. In the last decade, hundreds of thousands of people have taken advantage of the discounts available to them.

If you are in West Virginia — or are thinking about moving there — contact the Golden Mountaineer at:

West Virginia Golden Mountaineer
(304) 348-3317

GOOD SAM CLUB

Although age is not a factor in membership, the Good Sam Club is certainly an organization which has special appeal to those who are free to travel extensively.

Good Sam members are people who enjoy the

recreational vehicle lifestyle. There are some 2,000 local Good Sam chapters which have regular outings and entertaining activities. As an organization, Good Sam offers its members some expected and unexpected benefits.

From the standpoint of saving money, Good Sam members are eligible for special deals including discounts on gasoline, overnight camping, recreational vehicle parts and accessories, and propane gas purchases. If you are a member you can also get discounts that can be more than 50 percent on helpful publications, be protected by Good Sam's unique Emergency Road Service (pays the full cost of RV towing), and even purchase several lines of group insurance for you and your family.

Good Sam also offers services that are of special interest to people who enjoy getting away in their recreational vehicle. Along with the trip routing service, travelers checks, and credit card protection, they offer members specialty services like mail forwarding and a a way to reunite you with your pet if it gets lost during your travels.

Membership in the Good Sam Club costs $19 per year, $32 for two years and only $45 for three years. If you have any questions or wish to enroll by phone, you can call them at 1-800-234-3450.

GRAY PANTHERS

For over 20 years, the Gray Panthers have promoted the concept that all ages are of equal dignity and value. They reject the suggestion that dependence — whether of the young or old — constitutes inferiority.

They promote a social bill of rights that includes the provision of human services to all people in keeping with shared dignity. They also promote intergenerational cooperation in seeking equity and justice.

They are a true intergenerational group, so there is no minimum age for membership. Members can receive several publications; however, only their *Network* quarterly newspaper comes with membership. Other publications are available at an additional charge.

The fee for membership is $15 and you can choose to join either at a local or "at large" status. For more information, contact them at:

Gray Panthers
1424 16th St. NW, Suite 602
Washington, D.C. 20036
(202) 387-3111

INTERNATIONAL SENIOR CITIZENS ASSOCIATION

The International Senior Citizens Association (ISCA) is an independent organization which is open to all mature people regardless of nationality, race, creed or economic status. It functions as a world affairs forum for older persons in affiliation with the United Nations.

Members work to share the wisdom they have gained through maturity. The topics they are interested in are on both local and global scales covering everything from world peace to environmental issues.

This active group enjoys a tremendous brotherhood and keeps in touch through their quarterly newsletter, Biennial Borchardt International Festival, Annual Peace

Forum and Biennial International Conference. There is no minimum age for membership and dues are $6 for an individual and $30 for an organization.

For more information, contact:

Elaine Gordon, Administrative Director
1102 Crenshaw Blvd.
Los Angeles, CA 90019
(213) 857-6434

MATURE OUTLOOK

Mature Outlook is one of several discounting programs which are offered to mature shoppers by major retailers. This one is a member of the Sears Family of Companies.

Sears' motto, "Your money's worth and a whole lot more," is certainly true here. There are cash discounts and savings on health aids, travel, dining, and membership in the Allstate Motor Club.

From a cash standpoint, every year when you pay $9.95 to renew your Mature Outlook membership, you will receive $100 in "Sears Money." These coupons come in different denominations from $2 to $25 and can be used to reduce the prices of items you purchase either in the retail store or in the catalog. "Sears Money" can be used on regular priced or sale merchandise — it can not be used as payment on your SearsCharge or Discover Card account.

Your membership entitles you to save two different ways at the Optical Department at Sears. Details are in Chapter 6.

For travel benefits, you can save 20 percent on the cost of your room at over 1,000 participating Holiday

Inn or Crowne Plaza Hotels. You can also save 10 percent on the cost of your meal at the participating hotel restaurants. The discount does not apply to alcoholic beverages, gratuities, room service or tax. Be sure you present your Mature Outlook card when you are being seated so the host or hostess can calculate the savings for you (and your guest) before your bill is presented.

If you enjoy traveling, then this is the time of your life you are most likely to be able to pick up and go on short notice. Mature Outlook members are automatically enrolled in TravelAlert which makes last-minute tours, early-booking incentives, cruises and other vacation packages available to members at special services.

While you travel, you and your spouse are each covered by $5,000 in Allstate Accidental Death and Dismemberment Coverage Protection. Like all insurance policies, you will need to read the Certificate of Insurance for all the details.

While you are planning your trip, you can order Citicorp Travelers Checks with no service fee or markup. Then, when you are ready to go, you can choose from discounts at four car rental firms: Budget/Sears, National, Hertz and Avis.

Mature Outlook members receive two publications, *Mature Outlook*, a bimonthly, glossy, lifestyle magazine, and *Mature Outlook Newsletter*, an informational monthly newsletter. Each publication also contains or comes with advertising offers which can help you save money on everything from clothing to Christmas cards.

Membership is available to you as soon as you turn 50. To get more information about Mature Outlook call 1-800-336-6330, ext. 42. Or you can write them at:

148

Mature Outlook
6001 N. Clark Street
Chicago, IL 60660-9977

NATIONAL ALLIANCE OF SENIOR CITIZENS
The National Alliance of Senior Citizens was formed to support seniors who hold conservative views in both life and politics. The NASC was founded to respond to these views and has identified several major principles and policy goals in their literature including:

Policy Areas
1. The outrageous rise in inflation which destroyed the retirement income of millions of retired persons;
2. Crime - which impacts all Americans, but most severely harms the helpless and trusting; and
3. The reform of Social Security - working to protect them and other programs from being bankrupted by irresponsible political leaders and by those who do not deserve their benefits.

Some of the money-saving benefits you would be eligible for as a NASC member include:
- NASC Classic Visa Card for qualified members
- NASC Group Life Plan: permanent cash value life insurance
- NASC Discount Shopping Service
- Free NASC Family Pharmaceutical Membership for discount prescriptions

- Wholesale prices on eyeglasses and eyewear
- Free subscription to *The Senior Guardian*
- Discounts on vitamins, minerals and health care products
- 20% discounts on car rentals at Hertz, Avis, and National
- Hotel and motel discounts
- Access to NASC Auto Quoting Service
- Membership in NASC Preferred Traveler Programs
- NASC recommended investment programs

If this organization sounds like something you would like to learn more about, you can call them at 1-703-528-4380. If you want to have a try-out membership, they offer a free three-month membership. Annual dues are $10 per year per person or $15 per couple. For more information, write them at:

National Alliance of Senior Citizens
2525 Wilson Boulevard
Arlington, VA 22201

NATIONAL ASSOCIATION FOR RETIRED CREDIT UNION PEOPLE

If you are 50 or older and are in any way associated with a credit union, then you qualify for membership in the National Association for Retired Credit Union People (NARCUP). NARCUP is dedicated to serving the needs of prime-life credit union members who are approaching or experiencing retirement.

The membership includes many popular and money saving offerings including travel and insurance services.

There are also some unexpected benefits like discount brokerage services and life insurance for grandchildren.

The travel benefits include the use of a 24-hour travel service and a three percent rebate on pretax costs of commissionable travel booked through them. There are travel discounts through auto rental firms (Avis, Alamo, National and Hertz). Along with the discount rates you can get through their travel service, members can also receive a 10 percent discount at participating Quality Inns and 25 percent at participating Ramada Inns. For even more potential savings, members can purchase a Quest International hotel discount card for about 80 percent off its regular price. Quest members can get discounts of 50 percent on hotel rooms from many well-known hotels.

Travel benefits extend to several other areas including half-price purchase of the KOA Value Kard which entitles holders to 10 percent off the normal camping rate and discounts on renting condominiums at attractive vacation destinations.

Because of NARCUP's credit union tie-in, they have a special interest in helping members with their financial concerns. Members receive booklets to help them plan and manage their retirement as well as plan the disposition of their estate.

Along with a $1,000 Accidental Death and Dismemberment Insurance Policy each primary member automatically receives, members can purchase life insurance for themselves and/or their child or grandchildren who are age 14 or younger. Medicare supplement insurance and wellness insurance are also available.

In terms of ways to save money on your health needs, members and their families can get discounts of up to 50 percent on generic and brand-name prescription medications, vitamins, and nonprescription health care products through Medi-Mail (see Chapter 6). NARCUP members can also join the Eye Care Plan of America and receive substantial discounts by paying wholesale for eyewear.

Like other organizations, NARCUP has a membership magazine to keep members up-to-date on organization benefits. Their *Prime Times* is a lively, lifestyle-type magazine which is mailed to members homes four times a year.

Membership in NARCUP is only $7 per year. They also offer lifetime memberships with rates starting at $100 for an individual age 50-59, down to $25 for an individual ages 90-99, and free from age 100. To learn more about joining NARCUP, contact them at:

NARCUP, Inc.
P.O. Box 391
Madison, WI 53701

NATIONAL ASSOCIATION OF
RETIRED FEDERAL EMPLOYEES

The National Association of Retired Federal Employees (NARFE) is made up of 500,000 federal civilian retirees, current federal civilian employees with five years vested service as well as their spouses and survivors. NARFE has 1,700 chapters throughout the United States, Puerto Rico, Guam, the U.S. Virgin Islands, Panama and the Philippines. It is the only organization solely devoted to protecting the individual and family interests of civilians who have retired or will retire from federal service.

If you meet the membership requirements, you will find that they can help you understand you retirement annuities, health benefits, survivor benefits, and disability problems. There are a variety of group insurance programs which members can participate in. NARFE also maintains a close association with the Office of Personnel Management.

NARFE's primary objective is to sponsor and support legislation that protects your earned benefits if you are eligible to be a member. National dues are $12 and local chapter dues range from $3 to $6. There is no minimum age. For more information, write to:

National Association of Retired Federal
  Employees
1533 New Hampshire Avenue, N.W.
Washington, DC 20036
(202) 234-0832

NATIONAL COUNCIL ON THE AGING

While this is not an organization of mature Americans as the other groups are, it does welcome retirees to its membership. As a member, you will get information about — and have a chance to have input into — policy and program development on every issue affecting the quality of life for older Americans.

The National Council on the Aging is a diverse coalition of individuals and organizations in a wide range of fields including; health care professionals, adult day care providers, senior housing specialists, social workers, educators, volunteers, rural advocates, senior centers, hospitals and intergenerational programs.

This group has been the creative force behind many programs which may be familiar to you including Foster Grandparents and lunchtime meal programs. They have trained hundreds of Family Friends who give special attention and support to chronically ill children and their families. They have also brought seniors together with latchkey children in special after-school programs.

If you are a working professional interested in this organization, your annual dues will be $60. But as a full-time retiree, your annual dues will only be $30.

You can receive more information and a membership application by contacting them at:

The National Council on the Aging, Inc.
Dept. 5087
Washington, DC 20061-5087
1-800-424-9046

NATIONAL SENIOR SPORTS ASSOCIATION

If you enjoy golf, tennis and/or bowling and like to save money, then the National Senior Sports Association (NSSA) may be just what you have been looking for.

Their goal is to encourage physical and emotional health through active sports participation and to enable members to access quality resorts for tournaments at economical prices through off-season scheduling and group purchasing.

That might sound a little formal, but real fun is what they deliver. While there are some financial benefits, members say that the joy of travel coupled with the health and emotional values of active sports participation with a widening circle of old and new friends are their favorite benefits.

The minimum age for membership is 50, and there are active members at every age up through their 80's. They welcome married couples, singles, widows, widowers and never-marrieds. There have even been some "love matches" when individuals who shared more than just an enjoyment of their sport decided to get married.

Other benefits for NSSA members include:

- NSSA Tournaments and Recreational Events
- Sports Holidays Abroad
- Monthly *Senior Sports News*
- Awards and Prizes for Winners
- Golfers' Passport Discount
- NSSA Gold MasterCard
- Auto Rental Discounts at Hertz, National or Avis
- NSSA Sports Apparel
- Air Travel Assistance - includes automatic flight insurance, and complimentary beverage/headset coupons
- Member Relations

As a member, you will enjoy special package plans that enable you to pursue your sport at resorts you may have only dreamed of visiting. These events may take place here in America or in resort locations like Scotland, Ireland, Bermuda, the Bahamas, and Acapulco. While there, you will be able to participate in events grouped by skill levels (and nonplaying companions enjoy a full range of planned activities at each event).

Membership costs $25 per year (including your spouse if you are married). There are discounts for multiple year and lifetime memberships. To enroll, send your check or MasterCard/Visa account number, expiration date and signature along with your name, address to:

National Senior Sports Association
10560 Main Street, Suite 205
Fairfax, VA 22030

OLDER ADULT SERVICE AND INFORMATION SYSTEM

The Older Adult Service and Information System (OASIS) is a unique organization which offers a variety of educational, cultural and health promotional programs for adults age 60 and over. OASIS membership is free and the classes are free or at a minimal cost.

OASIS was initially funded by a grant from the Department of Health and Human Services, Administration on Aging, to demonstrate the feasibility of a public/private partnership. OASIS currently receives major support from the May Department Stores Company, The Jewish Hospital of St. Louis and Washington University School of Medicine.

OASIS promotes, sponsors and coordinates programs which intellectually culturally, and physically maintain and continue to develop the quality of life for members. The primary focus areas are the arts, humanities and health. Classes are held in May Company Stores or other convenient sites. Joint programming with other community resources enables members to have opportunities to enjoy the resources of the symphony, theater, dance, art and history museums.

Classes usually meet once a week for six to eight weeks and are one and a half to two hours long. At any given time, you could be enjoying classes in creative dramatics, drawing from sculpture, Italian for the traveler, water exercise and recent changes in Social Security and Medicare.

There are OASIS centers all across the continental U.S. from Boston to Los Angeles. You will find centers in Portland, Oregon, Denver, Houston, St. Louis, Chicago, Cleveland and many other cities. Since the May Company has many well respected retailers as part of their organization, you will need to contact the main OASIS office to determine if there is a program near you.

You can contact them at:

OASIS
7710 Carondelet Avenue, Suite 125
St. Louis, MO 63105
(314) 862-2933

THE RETIRED OFFICERS ASSOCIATION

The Retired Officers Association (TROA) is a fast-growing organization open to all men and women who are or have been commissioned or warrant officers in any of the seven uniformed services — Army, Navy, Air Force, Marine Corps, Coast Guard, Public Health Service and National Oceanic and Atmospheric Administration. You are also eligible if you are the widow or widower of a deceased member or of someone who would have qualified for membership.

Their goal is to maintain a strong national defense and preserve the earned entitlements and benefits of members of the uniformed service, their families and survivors.

As a member, you will be eligible for many money saving benefits including:

- Low-cost Group CHAMPUS/MEDICARE insurance supplements
- Retirement information, advice and assistance
- Post retirement job placement service
- Assistance for survivors
- Economical travel independently or on TROA group tours
- Group health and life insurance plans
- Scholarship loans and grants
- Automobile lease/purchase plan and extended auto warranty service
- Financial services

As a member you will receive TROA's *The Retired Officer* magazine monthly which is packed with articles about national defense and current affairs as well as military history, travel, humor, human interest, hobbies and second-career opportunities. Your membership also makes you welcome at any of the over 400 autonomous local groups of retired officers affiliated with the national organization. These people stay active in local and state affairs affecting the retired military community.

There is no minimum age for this organization, but

over 90 percent of the members are at least age 50. Dues are $20 for regular and $15 for auxiliary (widows and widowers of deceased members or people who would have been eligible for regular membership).

For more information, write to:

The Retired Officers Association
201 N. Washington Street
Alexandria, VA 22314-9975

Y.E.S.

The Y.E.S. (Years of Extra Savings) program through Montgomery Ward stores offers you a tremendous discounts in their stores and through programs affiliated with Y.E.S.

Y.E.S. gives you a chance to decide what will be on sale at Montgomery Ward stores on Tuesdays. With your club membership card and the 10 percent Tuesday Discount Pass you are entitled to 10 percent off the marked price of any regular or sale merchandise in the store. However, there are some exclusions and this offer does not apply to their clearance centers, food service, repair service or any merchandise purchased through the mail.

Of course, the discounts do not apply to sales tax, delivery, installation or service agreements. It is also not valid in license departments or auto service where separate Y.E.S. Club discounts apply (although it is good for auto-related merchandise such as tires, batteries, etc.).

The 10 percent Tuesday Discount Pass cards are good for two months each, and can be found in *Vantage*, the membership magazine. There is no limit on the number of times you can use the discount card — just that it always be on Tuesday.

The Auto Service Discount Pass also comes in the magazine. It is good for a 10 percent discount on these routine maintenance services; oil changes, wheel alignment, brake service, tune-ups, computerized engine analysis, and installation of shocks and struts. These discounts are available on Tuesday, Wednesday, and Thursday.

There are other auto related benefits you can access through Y.E.S. If you are in the market for a car, your discount on the Car/Puter Service will help you save money. The Car/Puter print-out tells you the dealer cost for the make, model, and options you want to help you negotiate a better deal.

If you want to rent a truck to help you move large or small loads, Hertz Penske will give Y.E.S. members a 13 percent discount on any size truck.

Y.E.S. offers you two ways to save on car rentals. First, you can save when you rent a car from Avis, Hertz or National Car Rental. Then, if you reserve a car through the Y.E.S. Club Travel Service, you receive a 10 percent rebate in addition to the already discounted rate.

You can access the Travel Service by telephone and make your travel reservations for airfare, lodging, rental car, cruises, tours and railway trips. When your travel is in the U.S., you are eligible to receive cash rebates after you have taken the trip.

Montgomery Ward's Y.E.S. program offers you a variety of ways to save money while you take care of your health. Some of them are even offered right in the stores.

At the optical departments in larger Montgomery Ward stores offer Y.E.S. members a 20 percent savings on prescription lenses, frames, and (where permitted by state law) contact lenses. This offer applies to regularly priced merchandise. However, you can not use your 10 percent Tuesday Discount Pass with this offer.

Many larger stores also have a Montgomery Ward Hearing Aid Center. If Y.E.S. members purchase a regularly priced hearing aid there, they receive an automatic $50 reduction on one — or $100 reduction on two hearing aids.

If you choose to purchase your hearing aid at one of the 3,300 Beltone locations world-wide, you will be entitled to a $50 rebate for purchasing one hearing aid or $100 rebate for purchasing two.

Another service available, but not in Montgomery Ward stores, is the shop-by-mail pharmacy program they have available through America's Pharmacy. You can save anywhere from 20 to 40 percent on your prescriptions, over-the-counter drugs and other health needs.

Y.E.S. members will find some other interesting ways that they can use their membership to save money.

When tax time rolls around, you can save 10 percent on tax preparation fees at their in-store income tax service. This is available from February 1 through April 15.

Double your pleasure — at the Montgomery Ward Engraving Department you can save 10 percent on engravable gifts and then save another 10 percent on the actual engraving.

It is the kind of clip job you like when you save 20

percent on the regular price of haircuts, and hair care services like permanents, tints and styling at Montgomery Ward Hair Salons.

If you get tired of the hassle of finding the wrapping paper, tape, card and then actually sitting down and wrapping the gift? Y.E.S. members find coupons good for free in-store gift wrapping in *Vantage* magazine.

As a membership magazine, *Vantage* also includes other special offers and programs which will help you to save money on goods and services you want.

All these benefits come with the $2.90 monthly membership fee and are available to customers age 55 or above. If you would be interested in learning more. Call toll-free 1-800-421-5396, or write them at:

> Y.E.S. Discount Club
> 200 N. Martingale Road
> Schaumburg, IL 60173-2096

MORE GOOD READING

You do not have to belong to an organization to find interesting magazines and newsletters who are targeting you as their reader. As publishers become more aware of your needs (not to mention your clout in the marketplace) they are initiating many different publications which they hope will win your loyalty.

Some of these publications are locally published and designed strictly for a local audience. They tend to be printed on newsprint paper and be about magazine size. They can be a source of good information about money-saving opportunities at local businesses. In addition, if you have ever thought you might be interested in writing for publication, many of these weekly and/or monthly publications will eagerly consider material you send them.

Some of them are available on newsstands or by subscription. Many others are available through what are known as "drops." These are places where you can find free copies. You may find these drops at grocery stores, senior centers, libraries and other places where people tend to congregate.

The magazines listed here are beautiful lifestyle magazines, full of information of special interest to you. They are available at newsstands or you can write to them at their address.

- *Golden Years*, The Lifestyle Magazine for a New Age — Do not let the term New Age fool you. This magazine is not about New Age phenomena like crystals and channeling you may have heard about. It is a lively, lifestyle magazine including celebrity profiles, travel, health, grandparenting, money and other topics. It had been published in Florida and has recently become available throughout the country. *Golden Years* is published bi- monthly. If you cannot find it at your local newsstand, write for more information to:

  Carol B. Hittner, Editor-in-Chief
  Golden Years
  233 E. New Haven Avenue
  Melbourne, FL 32901

- *New Choices: For the Best Years* is also a wonderful lifestyle magazine which targets the interests of people nearing or enjoying retirement. You can get it at most newsstands. For subscription information, contact:

New Choices
P.O. Box 1945
Marion, OH 43305-1945
(1-800-347-6969)

These are just a sample of the magazines which are vying for your attention. A trip to a local newsstand will undoubtedly turn up several more general interest magazines targeting you by age group. You will probably also see a number of special interest magazines which are devoted to you and your peers on everything from fashion to finance to hobbies. The clerks at your newsstand may be able to point some of them out to you — just ask!

CHAPTER 12:
READER'S REPLY

". . . Parting is such sweet sorrow."
William Shakespeare, **Romeo and Juliet***, 1594-95*

I hope *Deals & Discounts* has helped you find new and exciting ways to save money. Now I would appreciate it if you will take a few minutes to help me.

Do you know of a discount or promotional program targeting people age 50 or older that I missed? If so, please tell me a little about it, including the name and address of the store, company or agency where you found the program.

You can also help me by letting me know about any problems you have had when you were trying to use a discount or promotional program described in this book.

As a thank-you for your help, if you are the first one to give me the specific information, and I use it in a future edition, I will mail you a free copy of my next edition of *Deals & Discounts* as soon as it is published.

If you have a funny story about your use of discounts and I use it in my next book, you will get a copy too!

Please mail your comments to:

Donna G. Albrecht
Deals & Discounts
P.O. Box 21423
Concord, CA 94521

INDEX

170

NOTES

NOTES

NOTES

LOOK FOR THESE TITLES IN OUR
MATURE READER SERIES:

OVER 50 AND STILL COOKING!
Recipes for Good Health and Long Life

THE NUTRITION GAME:
The Right Moves if You're Over 50

THE ENCYCLOPEDIA OF GRANDPARENTING
Hundreds of Ideas to Entertain Your
Grandchildren

DEALS AND DISCOUNTS
If You're 50 or Older

START YOUR OWN BUSINESS
AFTER 50 — OR 60 — OR 70!
These People Did. Here's How:

I DARE YOU!
How to Stay Young Forever

THE BEGINNER'S ANCESTOR RESEARCH KIT